# THE WO...
## Assembly Poems

*Paul Cookson*

Pie Corbett was a primary teacher and headteacher. He worked in teacher training and was English Inspector in Gloucestershire. He advised the National Literacy Strategy, especially on teaching poetry, writing and grammar. He writes training materials and runs in-service across the country. Author of over a hundred books, a poet and story-teller, he spends much of his time irritating editors by not answering the phone because he is making up poems or dreaming.

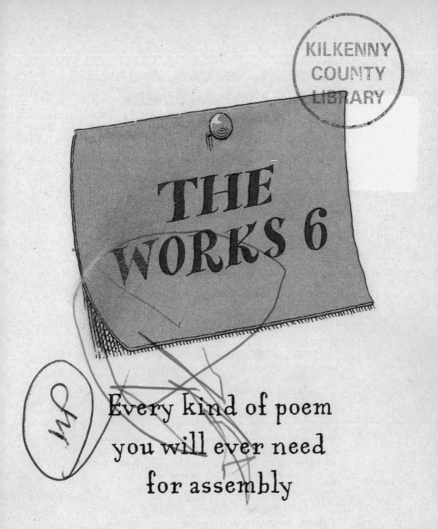

# THE WORKS 6

Every kind of poem
you will ever need
for assembly

Chosen by Pie Corbett

MACMILLAN CHILDREN'S BOOKS

To all those who cherish the human spirit –

rld; living with kindness.

*is no wealth but life'*

*John Ruskin, 1860*

First published 2007 by Macmillan Children's Books
a division of Macmillan Publishers Limited
20 New Wharf Road, London N1 9RR
Basingstoke and Oxford
www.panmacmillan.com

Associated companies throughout the world

ISBN: 978-0-330-43439-3

1 3 5 7 9 8 6 4 2

A CIP catalogue record for this book is available from
the British Library.

Typeset by IntypeLibra Limited
Printed and bound in Great Britain
by Mackays of Chatham plc, Kent

# Contents

# Contents

# Contents

# Contents

## Thoughts, Feelings and Faith

# Contents

# Contents

# Contents

# Contents

# Contents

# Contents

## People – Families and Friends, Heroes and Heroines

# Contents

## Looking After the World

# Contents

# Contents

## Celebrating Small Things

# Contents

# Contents

## The Journey – Growing, Changing, Old and New

# Contents

# Contents

## Signs, Stories and Symbols

# Contents

## Special Places

# Contents

# *Introduction*

When I began teaching, the headteacher told me that I was timetabled to take an assembly in three weeks' time. That date haunted me – in those days there were no 'help' books for taking assemblies. Let alone an anthology of poetry to dip into. I guess, in a way, this anthology has been on the cards ever since then.

Poems can be used in assemblies in many different ways.

- You might want to select a poem that can act as the main focus – introducing a theme or idea that you wish to explore.
- Or the poem might act as an enhancement to the main body of the assembly, possibly passing without comment.
- Some of these poems lend themselves to class performance – perhaps enhanced by the use of images, video, drama or the use of children's art to make a statement or present an idea.
- Many of the poems can be set to percussive or simple musical backing, to present them in a more memorable manner.
- Some of the celebratory poems might be used to establish a mood of contemplation and appreciation – a quiet and reflective moment.

While I was gathering these poems, I was struck by prayers from different religions that seemed to have a similar basis.

# Introduction

Indeed, after a while it became virtually impossible to tell which religion each prayer came from. I realized that at the core of our common humanity lay the human spirit, the vibrancy of our world and the idea that we are all a part of something larger, grander and greater – a concept of spiritual life.

Many of these poems celebrate with wonder the simple as well as the fantastic. Some poems raise issues to do with living together and coping with the modern world. Some act as a comfort and we may sit upon their shoulders and be carried through stormy times. Others will confront us with challenges. Many were gathered in schools or suggested by teachers and children. In particular, I tried to find some poems that might help us make sense of the more threatening and frightening moments, as well as the real need to break down barriers so that we learn to welcome all people as part of our world community.

Most children love communal singing, the sense of belonging and the uplift of beautiful words that are well spoken. The celebratory poems here may add a spark to uplift the human spirit as well as introducing a touch of awe and wonder at the beauty of our world. May we have happy assemblies that ignite the soul with joy and that bind us together in peace.

*Pie Corbett*

*Assembled Together*

## Lullaby

A heart to hate you
Is as far as the moon.
A heart to love you
Is as near as the door.

*Traditional Burundi*

## Assembled

Raindrops
race down the window pane,
leap into puddles.

The stream
bounces off rocks,
rushes to the lake.

The sea sucks in its breath,
breathes out.
The world is blue with water.

Here we are, a river of us, spilling
down corridors, flowing
into the hall, skidding to a stop.

Teachers walk a sea's edge
of crossed legs, shifting feet,
giggles, a foam of skirts.

At the clock-ticking end
we will flow again. Pouring
round adults

as if they are
the barnacled posts of a pier,
the bones of a wrecked ship.

*Mandy Coe*

# First Assembly

Teacher says that this morning
we are going to our first
Assembly.
I don't want to go to Assembly.
I didn't like the Tower of London much.
I won't like Assembly.
I have not got my money.
I have not got my packed lunch
or my swimming things . . .
And I don't want to go to Assembly.
    I want to stay here in my new school

I like my new school
I like my new teacher
I like my new friends
and the hamster.
I want to stay here.
Anyway –
I can't go to Assembly
because
Mum's collecting me after school
and we are going straight to
Tescos.

*Peter Dixon*

## Assembly

We assemble.
That's why it's called
assembly.
We sit cross-legged.
The area of the bottom
multiplied by the number of pupils
is greater than the area
of the hall floor.
We squiggle, we squeeze,
we squash, we squabble.
Jamie is asked to stay behind.
Behind is another word for bottom.

Miss walks on the stage.
So does Miss, Miss, Sir,
Miss, Sir, Miss, Miss and
Miss.

We have a talk about being good.
It is good to be good.
It is bad to be bad.
We will all be good.
We sing a song about trees.
The bone in my bottom
cuts into the floorboards.
I'm not worried about the floorboards.
Miss reads out the notices
but nobody notices.
We stand up.
I pull my bottom bone
out of the floorboards.
We line up like soldiers,
like prisoners, like refugees.

We file out
in a sensible manner.
The hall is now empty.
Except for Jamie.

*Steve Turner*

## *The Notices*

Here are the notices:

It has come to my attention
that Dumpty, in the green class,
has been climbing the wall.
This is against school rules.
If he's not careful, he'll fall.

The same applies to the hill.
Get your water from the tap,
not the well.
It's a dangerous place.
Ask Jack. Ask Jill.

Food is not to be eaten in class.
This includes Christmas pie
in the corner; take note, Jack Horner.
The tuffet, as I have stressed,
is still out of bounds.

Speaking of food brings me
to school dinners.
If, like Jack Sprat, you are on
a special diet, please inform
Mrs Hubbard in the canteen.
Low-fat meals are now available.

Items of cutlery have been disappearing.
I want this to stop.
No more excuses like:
'I didn't steal that spoon –
the dish ran away with it.'
It just doesn't wash.

There will be a parents' evening
next Wednesday in the main hall.
The title of the lecture is 'Cat Rescue'
and the speaker will be Tommy Stout.
Music will be performed by
Little Boy Blue and the King Cole Fiddlers.

Finally, a word about dress.
The following items are not
part of the school uniform:
dusty skirts, rabbit skin,
trousers with knee buckles,
nightgowns. With this in mind,
would the following please stay behind:
Shaftoe, Flinders, Bunting, Winkie.

*Steve Turner*

## Spring Assembly

Right! As you all know,
It's spring pretty soon
And I want a real good one this year.
I want no slackers. I want SPRING!
That's S-P-R-I-N-G! Got it?
Spring! Jump! Leap!
Energy! Busting out all over!
Nothing so beautiful! Ding-a-ding-a-ding!

Flowers: I want a grand show from you –
Lots of colour, lots of loveliness.
Daffodils: blow those gold trumpets.
Crocuses: poke up all over the parks and gardens,
Yellows, purples, whites; paint that picture.
And a nice show of blossom on the fruit trees.
Make it look like snow, just for a laugh,
Or loads of pink candy floss.

Winds: blow things about a bit.
North, South, East, West, get it all stirred up.
Get March nice and airy and exciting.

Rain: lots of shimmering showers, please.
Soak the earth after its winter rest.
Water those seeds and seedlings.
And seeds: start pushing up.
Up! Up! Up! Let's see plenty of green.

Sunshine: give the earth a sparkle
After the rain. Warm things up.

And you birds: I haven't forgotten you.
Fill the gardens with song.
Build your nests (you'll remember how).
And you lambs: set an example,
Jump, leap, bound, bounce, spring!

And kids: ditch those coats and scarves,
And get running and skipping.
Use that playground; none of this
Hanging about by the school wall
With your hands in your jeans pockets.
It's spring, I tell you.
And you're part of it
And we've got to have a real good one this year.

*Gerard Benson*

## Rowdy Kids

When we were all assembled
The Head turned red and trembled
And said that we resembled

A misbehaving tidal wave,
The row when monkeys rant and rave,
A rockfall echoed round a cave,

Seagull clamour, ringtone stammer,
Workmen wielding saw and hammer,
Shopping-centre muzak yammer,

A zoo afraid, a bombing raid,
The way that mules and donkeys brayed,
The whine which dental drills all made,

A sonic boom around the room,
The wail of sinners sensing doom,
A choir of ghosts within their tomb,

A thunderstorm in uniform,
A bunch of bees that form a swarm,
Dragons killing a unicorn,

Some seismic quakes, a squeal of brakes,
Big bawling babes with bellyaches,
The sound a squad of sirens makes,

The tortured vowel when wild wolves howl,
An old tyrannosaurus growl,
The din of dogs that yap and yowl,

Though no one heard a word he said.
Our row was louder than the Head,
So we just read his lips instead.

*Nick Toczek*

## I Think I'm the Only One

I think I'm the only one
who closes my eyes for the prayers in assembly
but I can't be sure . . .
because I think I'm the only one
who closes my eyes for the prayers in assembly.

*Paul Cookson*

## God's Aid

God to enfold me,
    God to surround me,
God in my speaking,
    God in my thinking.

God in my sleeping,
    God in my waking,
God in my watching,
    God in my hoping.

God in my life,
    God in my lips,
God in my soul,
    God in my heart.

God in my sufficing,
  God in my slumber,
God in mine ever-living soul,
  God in mine eternity.

*Traditional Celtic*

# Festivals, Celebrations and Seasons

## After St Augustine

Sunshine let it be or frost,
Storm or calm, as thou shalt choose;
Though thine every gift were lost,
Thee thyself we could not lose.

*Mary Coleridge*

## Thaw

The white garden
softens to green again
and cries silently.

Water music
splashes from guttering.
The gull has lost that

puzzled look. When
the cat wakes and stretches
he'll be free at last.

We'll see him soon,
curious and sly at the
end of the garden.

The earth did not
die of some white disease.
It's warm! It breathes!

*Fred Sedgwick*

# The Chinese Dragon

I'm the dragon who dances in the street.
I'm the dragon in the festival.
I leap and twist on caterpillar feet.
I'm the dragon who dances in the street.
I snap and snort and stamp to the beat.
I shiver my scales. I can't keep still.
I'm the dragon who dances in the street.
I'm the dragon in the festival.

I'm the dragon of red and green and gold.
I'm King of the Chinese New Year.
I come from the land of stories of old.
I'm the dragon of red and green and gold.
I can breathe out fire or smoke that's cold.
If you've been good then you've nothing to fear
From the dragon of red and green and gold –
The King of the Chinese New Year.

*Catherine Benson*

# *Dragon*

The dragon's face is wrinkled and the deep lines shape a
mad grin
It bobs up and down on poles outside the door of the Ma
Bo cafe
The great red and golden head nods and shakes towards
the pressing
crowd of people like a bull tossing away annoying flies,
his tail ripples and sways above the knobbly mass of their
heads
as if he was slithering through a bank of pebbles, a riverbed.

In the window hangs a row of red cooked chickens and at
the door
the cook and his customers lean out and yell encouragment:
the dragon makes up his mind, lifts his head to the crowd's
roar,
rises to the bait, the dangling strings of red paper money,
the green packets of rice parcelled neatly in leaves,
and taking the gifts gives good luck for the next year.

So everyone cheers, and the cymbals crash louder than ever
as he heaves
and surges onward, and the curled crackers crackle in a
fearful ear-
splitting rat-tat-tat like machine-gunfire. And through the
thunderous sea
the dragon of good fortune dances forward with fierce glee.

*Dave Calder*

## Cinquain Prayer, February Night

On this
cold night I kneel
with thanks for catkins, pale
green under the lamplight by the
roadside.

*Fred Sedgwick*

## Loving Gertie Best

I love Hannah's hairstyle
And Danuella's dress.
I love Chloe's class – she is
A clear catwalk success –

*But Gertie gets me giggling
And I love Gertie best.*

I love Rita's writing,
I love Zara's art.
The music Maisie plays with Pol
Hammers in my heart –
I hear it from the north, the south,
The east and from the west –

*But Gertie gets me giggling*
*And I love Gertie best.*

I love Maggie's movement
When she's jiving in the gym.
I love Sabrina's soft goodnight
When disco lights are dim.
I love the way that Pippa passes
Every little test –

*But Gertie gets me giggling*
*And I love Gertie best.*

I love Eram's glossy hair,
I love Nasima's nose.
I love Farida's fingers
And her brightly painted toes.
I love Niamh and Norma
When I'm feeling sad and stressed –

*But Gertie gets me giggling*
*And I love Gertie best.*

*Fred Sedgwick*

## Shrove Tuesday Haiku

In the kitchen peeling
pancakes    from    the    ceiling
                like frail                frisbees.

*Ginna Macklin*


## A Prayer for Lent

For all I have said
and should not have said,

For all I have done
and should not have done,

For all I have thought
and should not have thought,

I am sorry.

*David Harmer*

# *Lent*

This year I'm giving up time –

Time to keep my bedroom clean,
Time to clear the kitchen table,
Time to sweep the backyard,
Time to help when I am able.

Time to do my homework,
Time to run down to the shops,
Time to carry heavy bags,
Time to help Mum when she stops –

And sits down for a cup of tea –
Time to give others time,
And in the end, some time for me.

*David Lucas*

## The Doll Festival

Lighted lanterns
cast a gentle radiance
on pink peach blossoms.

Third day of third month.
Mother brings out five long shelves –
black lacquer, red silk.

On the topmost shelf
we place gilded folding screens
and the two chief dolls.

They are Emperor
and Empress, in formal robes:
gauzes, silks, brocades.

On the lower steps,
court ladies with banquet trays,
samisen players.

High officials, too,
kneeling in solemn stillness:
young noble pages.

Fairy furniture –
dressers, mirrors, lacquer bowls,
bonsai, fans, braziers.

Should the royal pair
wish to go blossom-viewing –
two golden palanquins.

Third day of third month.
Our small house holds a palace –
we are its guardians.

Lighted lanterns
cast a gentle radiance
on pink peach blossoms.

*James Kirkup*

## Holi

At the festival of fun.
Our faces are streaked
with rainbows.

We giggle,
toasting each other
with milkshakes;
chewing sweet roast coconut.

*Bashkar Chakravati*

## Purim

Hiss and boo,
and stamp your feet.
Shake your rattle –
Blotting out the name
Of Haman –

And cheer for the battle
Fought by brave Esther.

*Sal Berum*

## Half-Term

One day to start on your homework,
One day to mess around,
One day to tidy your bedroom,
One day to shop in town.
One day to be baked by the sunshine,
One day to be soaked by the wet.
One day to visit the dentist,
The hairdresser and the vet.
One day to finish that homework,
One day to see your friend –
Half-term's hardly started,
Before it's come to an end.

*Penny Dolan*

## Mad March Sun

Woods were waking up today
after the snow.
Twigs stretched away winter stiffness,
ticked dry
in the mad March sun.

Mists rolled along ribbed fields.
Warmed from wetness
they dressed a threadbare hedge
as black scraps of boasting crows
called taunts across the sky's playground.

*Gina Douthwaite*

## The Birthday of Buddha

With my elder brother and younger sister
I, the youngest son, Chiaki, aged eleven,
accompany father, mother, elder sister
to the small temple at the end of our street.

At the other end of our street hangs like an old
wood-block print, beyond the grey tiled roofs
of little shops and houses, our divine Mount Fuji –
a lucky omen for this holy day – for Fuji-san
too often hides himself in smog or clouds.
But today the lingering last snows on his sacred peak
are sparkling in the pure blue heavens.

We are all wearing our best clothes –
my mother and sisters in bright spring kimono and zori,
we three men in good suits, shirts, ties, shoes.
But my father's carrying a folding paper fan.

At the temple gate, the smiling priest
bows his welcome, and we all bow deeply in return.
He sometimes plays baseball with us, but today
he is wearing formal robes.

We bow to the statue of the infant Buddha
standing inside his miniature temple
of spring greenery and pale-rose cherry-blossom.
He is shining in the happy sun. One by one,
we slowly pour over him ladles of sweet brown tea.
He always seems to enjoy it. He, too, is smiling.

The priest and his wife and children invite us
to take tea, the same festive tea we gave the Buddha,
with sweet cakes, satsumas and candies.

With folded hands, we bow farewell to Buddha,
and to the smiling priest, who bows farewell to us.

– But once outside the temple gate
 my older brother and I dash home to change our clothes
for baseball practice in the field behind the temple,
where the infant Buddha goes on smiling
as if he, too, is on our team.

And at the end of our street, old Fuji-san
hangs like a crimson half-moon in the afterglow.

*James Kirkup*

## Palm Sunday

In our porch
there are palm crosses –

one for each year
that we've lived here –

whenever I come home
they are there –

frail reminders

of Jesus riding
into Jerusalem

on the donkey's bare back

and palm leaves scattered
like confetti

on the dusty streets

and I hear the steady clip
of the donkey's hooves

passing by.

*Pie Corbett*


## Ass

Ass they all called me
Just part of the furniture,
Never had a name.

Long-ears they called me,
Not the sort of face you'd put
In a fancy frame!

Old friend they called me.
On the road to Bethlehem
That's what I became.

*Sue Cowling*

## Easter Monday

We tied the white eggs in onion skin,
Wrapped them round with string.
We boiled them for so long
The water looked like strong tea.
Lifted out, the string was a dirty khaki,
But the eggs – the eggs were glorious
Marbled brown, amber and yellow.

When we were at the top of the hill,
When the others rolled theirs down to crack,
I held mine back –
It was too beautiful.

*Catherine Benson*

## Easter

When Jesus rode at Easter
into Jerusalem
a crowd cried out, '*Hosanna!*'
I was one of them.

When Jesus prayed at Easter
in dark Gethsemane,
his friends all failed to stay awake –
I was of that company.

When Jesus stood at Easter
accused and put on trial
his friends all fled and turned away –
and I fled too – I ran a mile.

When Jesus died at Easter
The day the sky turned black,
I wept at the sin and waste of it
and longed to bring him back.

When Jesus rose at Easter –
new life from death's cruel tree –
my heart broke with the joy of it
for this was done for me.

*Jan Dean*

## Good Friday

In Painswick,

we wore thorny crowns

and circled round the church,
holding hands

like one family
in a daisy chain of children,
parents and pensioners –

then Poppy, Daisy and Teddy
crouched by a tombstone
to shelter from the wind

and we ate
sweet currant buns
imprinted with a cross

to remind ourselves

of the loss

*Pie Corbett*


## Mother's Day

I'm making breakfast for my mum, the kind she likes the
   most.
An egg and milky coffee and a round of buttered toast.
The egg is boiling nicely. It needs just ten seconds more,
Then I'll . . . Brrring, brrring, brrring brrring! 'Hello, it's
   Di next door.'

Natter natter natter natter natter natter natter.
Chatter chatter chatter chatter chatter chatter chatter.

The egg's had seven minutes but I don't suppose it's
  spoiled.
I know a lot of people who prefer their eggs hard-boiled.
The coffee won't take very long. The milk is in the pan,
So I'll . . . Brrring, brrring, brrring brrring! 'Hello, dear, it's
  your gran.'

Natter natter natter natter natter natter natter.
Chatter chatter chatter chatter chatter chatter chatter.

The milk's boiled dry. I'll have to make some lemon tea
  instead,
But I can't find any lemons, so I think I'll toast the bread.
The slice is cut, the grill is hot, it won't be long until
I can . . . Brrring, brrring, brrring brrring! 'Hello, it's Uncle
  Bill.'

Natter natter natter natter natter natter natter.
Chatter chatter chatter chatter chatter chatter chatter.

*My* turn to make a phone call. I dial the Fire Brigade.
'The toast's on fire! Come quickly, please – and bring some
  marmalade.'

*Julia Donaldson*

## Mother's Day Prayer

Dear God
Today is Mother's Day.
Please make her backache go away.

May her pot plants all grow healthy
and a lottery win make her wealthy.

May our dad buy her some flowers
and take us all to Alton Towers.

May her fruitcake always rise
and the sun shine bright
in her blue skies.

*Roger Stevens*

# *April 1st*

Our teacher's looking nervous,
I think she's feeling tense –
sixty eyes all watch her closely,
we're tingling with suspense.
She shrewdly tests her chair seat,
before daring to sit down –
her eyes flick, spy-like, round the room
under a worried frown.
She peers into her pencil pot
as if it's going to bite –
and slowly takes her pencil out
to check before she writes.
Our thirty watchful faces
all tell that something's up –
then her attention fastens
on her waiting coffee cup.
'I think I'll leave my coffee,
till after registration,
I apologize if this frustrates
your keen anticipation!'
She opens up the register,
says, 'It's very quiet in school . . .'
then out it jumps, and she screams, 'AAAARGH!'
and we scream, 'APRIL FOOL!'

*Liz Brownlee*

# Hunting the Leaven
### *(for Passover)*

Take a candle, take a feather,
hunt in every crack.
Find each piece of leavened food
and quickly bring it back.

We'll clean our home from top to bottom,
clear out all the yeast.
And then we'll lay the table
for our special Seder feast.

*Tony Mitton*

# Baisakhi

Crystals of sugar
   swirl
as the sword
   stirs Amrit.

Listening to the tale
of the Five Beloved Ones,

who dodged death
by giving their lives
to God.

*Anon.*

## *The Dragon Who Ate Our School*

The day the dragon came to call,
She ate the gate, the playground wall
And, slate by slate, the roof and all,
The staffroom, gym and entrance hall,
And every classroom, big or small.

So . . .
She's undeniably great.
She's absolutely cool,
The dragon who ate
The dragon who ate
The dragon who ate our school.

Pupils panicked. Teachers ran.
She flew at them with wide wingspan.
She slew a few and then began
To chew through the lollipop man,
Two parked cars and a transit van.

Wow . . . !
She's undeniably great.
She's absolutely cool,
The dragon who ate
The dragon who ate
The dragon who ate our school.

She bit off the head of the head.
She said she was sad he was dead.
He bled and he bled and he bled.
And as she fed, her chin went red
And then she swallowed the cycle shed.

Oh . . .
She's undeniably great.
She's absolutely cool,
The dragon who ate
The dragon who ate
The dragon who ate our school.

It's thanks to her that we've been freed.
We needn't write. We needn't read.
Me and my mates are all agreed,
We're very pleased with her indeed.
So clear the way, let her proceed.

Cos . . .
She's undeniably great.
She's absolutely cool,
The dragon who ate
The dragon who ate
The dragon who ate our school.

There was some stuff she couldn't eat.
A monster forced to face defeat,
She spat it out along the street –
The dinner ladies' veg and meat
And that pink muck they serve for sweet.

But . . .
She's undeniably great.
She's absolutely cool,
The dragon who ate
The dragon who ate
The dragon who ate our school.

*Nick Toczek*


## The Estuary Field Trip

I walked with my class along the estuary
The salty wind sneaked through the cracked concrete
of time-worn sea defences,
stirred the weeds and rusty wire
that rose from the caked mud bed.
Thirty children poked under rocks
hunting for crabs
and tugged at a lump of driftwood,
perhaps once part of a sailing barge
taking bricks to London.

Isn't it beautiful? I said
Richard looking at me, nodded, smiled
A rare moment
A mystical union of teacher and pupil
Mr Stevens, said Richard,
Did you see the Man U game last night?

*Roger Stevens*

# Lord of All Gardens
*Kyrielle*
*for Rebecca Moore on the occasion of her*
*first communion, 10 June 2001*

The garden's soaked in sunlight where,
Marooned in my mortality,
I stand and murmur common prayer:
Lord of all gardens, pray for me.

Mysteriously float the scents
Of herb and flower, grass and tree.
The cat hunts slyly by the fence.
Lord of all gardens, pray for me.

Where the sky above me stands
Clouds' silent music's drifting free.
My mind is still. So are my hands.
Lord of all gardens, pray for me.

With the wide world, or all alone;
Whether in air, on land or sea,
My heart won't turn to sand or stone –
Lord of all gardens, pray for me.

*Fred Sedgwick*

## Christening Gift

The gift I bestow is last but not least –
A permanent magical feast,
A path to knowledge, a key to learning
That grows with you at each year's turning,
A thousand stories for your pleasure,
Jokes and prayers in equal measure,
Conversation and songs for singing,
Poems for the joy of wild words ringing.
I grant you a life spent under its spell.
Words are my gift – use them well.

*Sue Cowling*

## Be Tall, Thomas
*for Thomas Alexander Harrison on the
occasion of his baptism*

Be tall, Thomas, be tall.
Thrive strong and straight,
Become a joyful soul
As wide and open to the sky
As buttercups in sun
Or the day's eye shining in the grass.
Revel in the wonder of it all,
Rejoice. Grow. Laugh.
Be tall in spirit, tall in giving

Generous and brave –
For all of this is in you;
Every good impulse that has ever been
Every sudden hope and every prayer
That moves through this created world
Is there.
In you God flows
And in his work of grace you have a share.
Be tall, Thomas, be tall.
There are no limits
To what love in you can do.

*Jan Dean*

# My Card for Father's Day

This is the card that I've made for my dad.
It's sticky with glue . . . but it's not too bad.

I cut out this ship and then stuck it in
And I drew this shark with a great big fin.

Then I've written as neatly as I can
'With love to my dad. He's the world's best man!'

This is the card that I'll give to my dad.
It's sticky with glue . . . but it's not too bad.

*Wes Magee*

## Poems to the Sun

All the cattle are resting in the fields,
The trees and the plants are growing,
The birds flutter above the marshes,
Their wings uplifted in adoration,
And all the sheep are dancing.
All winged things are flying,
They live when you have shone on them.

The boats sail upstream and downstream alike,
Every highway is open because you dawn.
The fish in the river leap up in front of you,
Your rays are in the middle of the great green sea.

*Traditional*
*(Ancient Egypt)*

## Great sun

Great sun
Eat the clouds up
So that my love can flourish with my garden,
So that my love, my love
And all the busy joy of greenery
Can flourish.

Storm wind
That brings the clouds
Huge and heavy, stifling up the heavens,
Push on, push them over
So that the flattened garden can be righted
And love recover.

*Jenny Joseph*


## *Zenith – hold it*

Cuckoo long gone
Summer heat upon
The land;
Harvest not yet come.

Waiting, who knows for what
To happen, at the spot
In time
We have arrived at.

If we could – Stop momentarily.
Let ourselves be
Held, moveless, in the turning hub
Of eternity.

*Jenny Joseph*

# The Longest Day of the Year

It is the longest day of the year.
Extra daylight hours
That I could use for inspiration
To write a poem celebrating
The longest day of the year.

It is the longest day of the year
And here I am, stuck inside,
Writing a poem about it being
The longest day of the year
When really I want to go out.

The sun is shining,
There's not a cloud in the sky,
The birds are singing
And the longest day of the year
Should be a good day for poems.
But it isn't.

It's a good day to take off your socks,
Paddle in the sea,
Make sandcastles,
Eat the largest ice cream you can find
And maybe, just maybe,
Maybe write a poem in the sand
For the waves to wash away.

*Paul Cookson*

## One Moment in Summer

The house is dropping swallows
one by one from under the gutter

they swoop and fall
on our heads as we queue
for ice cream.

It is so hot
that the long line of cars clogging the road
hum like a line of electric fires.

They shine and shimmer, stink of oil and warm seats
the children gaze out from their misted windows.

Trapped under glass
hair plastered down with sweat
gasping for breath like frogs under ice.

The cars crawl round the curve
of the road, stuck in between the shop
and the cafe.

My ice cream is butterscotch and almond
Lizzie's is chocolate, Harriet's vanilla.

They are so delicious and cold
we lick them slowly, letting the long, cool flavours
slide down our tongues.

Inside the cars, the red-faced people
begin to boil.

The swallows flit and dart
rapid specks of blueblack and white
the summer flies at us
like an arrow.

*David Harmer*

## Mela

Listen to the reading,
  listen to the hymn.
Today it is a holy day.
  Let us think of him
who guided us
  and brought us
from darkness
  into light –
into sudden morning
  out of thick night.

Let us eat together.
  Let us take our ease.
Let us throw our weapons down.

Here, is peace.

*Jean Kenward*

## Mela Menagerie

It was summertime,
the animals were having a mela.
    The elephants cooked
curried pumpkin with tikka masala,
    sun-shy frogs and mice
sheltered under the hood of a cobra,
    bears and cockatoos
swapped couplets in a mini mushaira,
    horses and camels
pranced and danced a fantastic bhangra,
    tigers took pot shots
at juicy papayas for one paisa,
    lions showed off paws
decorated with delicate henna,
    donkeys for a laugh
crowned a mule their day-long Maharaja,
    pelicans swallowed
swords with mango chutney and paratha,
    Sinbad's ship sailed in
on waves of dolphin abracadabra,
    monkeys built bridges
recalling how they once helped Prince Rama,
    while Ali Baba
and forty rooks acted out life's drama.
    It was summertime,
the animals were having a mela.

*Debjani Chatterjee*

49

## End of Term

At last the term is over
And we all say Hooray
And everyone is looking forward
To the holiday

Next term we'll all be older
And in another class
We learnt a lot of useful things
And time went by so fast

And so we say a last goodbye
Put on our hats and coats
We wave to Miss Moss at the gate
And a lump is in our throats

Because Frog Class is the best class
I thought you'd like to know
But right now – what are we waiting for?
It's the holiday
Let's go!

*Roger Stevens*

## Last Day

This class was special.

No one was particularly clever,
Particularly naughty,
Particularly messy,
Particularly anything.

Nothing miraculous happened,
Nothing stunning,
Or funny, or frightening, or strange.

Each day was much like another
As the year crept softly by,
Leaving its ordinary debris
Of drawings and stories
And small successes
And unremarkable memories.

Yet something hung between us,
Something that glittered like chalk dust
On a sunny day.

It was nothing you could touch,
Or capture,
Or exactly define,
But when I see the scattered offerings
Left on my desk –

A necklace of shells,
A giant pot of talcum
Smelling of yesterday,
A limp bunch of yellow flowers,
A crumpled card
Signed with love –
I can hardly bear
To walk away.

This class was special.

*Clare Bevan*

# Leavers' Song

When I know that something's wrong
Can I change it? Am I strong?
Will I hesitate, or dither or delay?
When I see there is a need
To combat somebody's greed
Can I face it, or just turn the other way?
When I hear my inner voice
Say I have no other choice,
(Even though I do not want to but I ought)
Will I say 'enough's enough'!
Will I make believe I'm tough?
That I'm made of stronger metal than I thought?
*Can I say out loud*

*I make me feel proud?*
*Would I like to be*
*Someone just like me?*
*When I say goodbye*
*Will I think that I*
*Made a difference to any one of you.*
When the odds are stacked against me,
When the writing's on the wall,
When it seems that all my friends have turned from me,
Will I falter, will I alter
My belief in what is true
When I know that I am right to disagree?

Can I face the bully down
Will I give away my love?
Will I be a friend to strangers as I go?
Will I make the perfect choice
Not be selfish, not be mean,
Be the kind of person that I want to know?
*Can I say out loud*
*I make me feel proud?*
*Would I like to be*
*Someone just like me?*
*When I say goodbye*
*Will I think that I*
*Made a difference to any one of you.*

*Vicki Johnson*
*Northwood Primary School*

## Recipe for a Summer Holiday

Take a stretch of sandy beach
And a calm sea.
Add a pier, a promenade,
donkey rides and a funfair.
Sprinkle with buckets and spades,
deckchairs, lilos and picnic baskets.
Cover with thick slices of sunshine
And wrap in warm photographs
To look at on dark winter days.

*John Foster*

## Prayer for the First Day of the School Holidays

Dear God . . . please . . .

Let rain be banished and the sun be strong
Let time pass slowly and the days be long

Let laughter echo forever with friends
Let fun and games be without end

May good days be many and bad days be few
May parents not find odd jobs for you

May bikes be indestructible and balls not be lost
May day trips be bountiful whatever the cost

May school be something we never remember
Let it always be August and never September

Thanks
Amen

*Paul Cookson*

## Seaside Song

It was a
sun-boiled, bright light, fried egg, hot skin, sun-tanned
sssizzzzzzler of a day.

It was a
pop song, ding-dong, candy floss, dodgem car, arcade, no
shade
smashing seaside town.

We had
a well time, a swell time, a real pell-mell time,
a fine time, a rhyme time, a super double-dime time.

We
beach swam, ate ham, gobbled up a chicken leg,
climbed trees, chased bees,
got stuck in sand up to our knees,
played chase, flew in space,
beat a seagull in a skating race,
rowed boats, quenched throats,
spent a load of £5 notes,
sang songs, hummed tunes,
played hide and seek in sandy dunes.

Did all these things
too much by far
that we fell asleep going back in the car
from the seaside.

*John Rice*

## Krishna's Birthday

At midnight –

tinsel glistens –
lights glitter –
stars glimmer –

the baby Krishna rocks
in a cradle.

*Samatananda*

## Problems with Hurricanes

A campesino looked at the air
And told me:
With hurricanes it's not the wind
or the noise or the water.
I'll tell you he said:
it's the mangoes, avocados
Green plantains and bananas
flying into town like projectiles.
How would your family
feel if they had to tell
The generations that you
got killed by a flying
Banana?

Death by drowning has honour
If the wind picked you up
and slammed you
Against a mountain boulder
This would not carry shame
But
to suffer a mango smashing
Your skull
or a plantain hitting your
Temple at 70 miles per hour
is the ultimate disgrace.

The campesino takes off his hat –
As a sign of respect
towards the fury of the wind
And says:
Don't worry about the noise
Don't worry about the water
Don't worry about the wind –
If you are going out
beware of mangoes
And all such beautiful
sweet things.

*Victor Hernandez Cruz*


# The First Day After the Holidays

Is always the best.
You get to see all your friends again
and catch up on the news.

Nobody does much work,
just writing your name on a new exercise book
and nobody sets homework.

You don't get told off
for not having your PE kit
and the breaks are often longer.

Yes, the first day after the holidays
is always the best,
apart from the day we break up.

On the second day
it always feels like you've never been away
and holidays seem an eternity ago.

*Paul Cookson*

## First Day

First day
feeling new
don't know what
to say or do

First day
feeling funny
by the door
cling to mummy

First day
feeling shy
really trying
not to cry

First day
feeling wrong
morning seems
so very long

First day
feeling strange
don't know
anybody's name

First day
out the gate
back tomorrow –
can't wait!

*James Carter*


## It's Not What I'm Used To

I don't want to go to Juniors . . .

The chairs are too big.
I like my chair small, so I fit
Exactly
And my knees go
Just so
Under the table.

And that's another thing –
The tables are too big.
I like my table to be
Right
For me
So my workbook opens
Properly.
And my pencil lies in the space at the top
The way my thin cat stretches into a long line
On the hearth at home.

Pencils – there's another other thing.
Another problem.
Up in Juniors they use pens and ink.
I shall really have to think

About ink.

*Jan Dean*

## First Day

I stand at the front in autumn clothes
While children shuffle past in rows.

Who will be mine? The scruffy crowd
Who wriggle and giggle and talk too loud?
The gangly boy with the coconut hair?
The angry child with the angry stare?
The silent girl who stands alone,
Face as blank as a polished stone?
The fidgets, the dreamers, the clumsy crew?
The ones who scratch and the ones who chew?
The ones with eyes rubbed sore and red?
The ones who fill my soul with dread?
Their names are called. Too late to pray.
My fate is sealed. They turn my way.

And the gangly boy who leads the queue
Says, 'All of us hoped we'd be with you.'

*Clare Bevan*

## Teacher's Prayer, September

*'But he who kisses the joy as it flies*
*Lives in eternity's sunrise'*
                    *William Blake*

Lord
        as earth re-colours
    itself from bright to brown
and winds distress the narrow streets

    of this east English town
and smoke is drifting from the fields
    and mists shroud every hill
and conkers start to tumble

    and nights come soon and chill
Lord
        may the children listen
    may Ofsted stay away
may silver pieces that I earn
    (please!) last until payday

and may the children learn, Lord
    and may I too be wise
and learn to live as they live
    in eternity's sunrise

                    *Fred Sedgwick*

# An 'Indian Summer'

September – and I see the urban fisherfolk
dreaming of salmon leaping in roaring rivers.

Sunday in Sheffield – and I walk by the canal.
The high Himalayas drum with roaring rivers.

The dragonfly flits in the Yorkshire afternoon
while Mandakini descends in roaring waters.

Once a laughing goddess roamed along these banks;
now unknown, her name resounds through roaring waters.

Ducks swim, ruffling their feathers over this landscape.
Yards away, industry storms its roaring waters.

Whatever she is called, Ganga meditates
on summer rippling the calm of English rivers.

*Debjani Chatterjee*

## Distributing the Harvest

We collapsed the tableau carefully,
passing it piece by piece to a class
of kids, arms held up to make their bids
for brussels, for solid and sensible spuds
to ballast the base of baskets.
The eggs looked on from safe distance
while tomatoes split their skins and sticky
apples slipped and rolled across the polished floor
to be challenged and captured and pushed
into bags, now swollen fat with harvest swag,
until all that remained were laid-back marrows,
stout heroes of the garden patch.

Then burdens were lifted, shouldered and
shifted, till like some desert caravan of
Oriental kings with gifts, our harvest bearers
struggled out, towards the town, across the bridge.
Later we heard of casualties, someone's
cucumber spun under a car, while others on
the farthest run found no one home and hauled
it back or posted produce through letter flaps,
but then we knew nothing of that;
we heard instead, all afternoon, news of
successful missions and watched returning faces,
bright as harvest moons.

*Brian Moses*

# Remembrance Day Remembered

For the sake of men we never knew
We trooped into the hall
Where their names in golden letters
Were written on the wall.

Somebody sounded a bugle
And ghosts seemed everywhere
Until the last note softly fell
On the suddenly empty air.

Then the world filled up with living
In its own accustomed way,
With the usual busy traffic
Of the usual busy day.

But what I most remember
And know that I always will
Is how we stood utterly silent
And absolutely still.

*John Mole*

## Kathina

The monks sit cross-legged
        still
        as stones

their hands pressed together
like the pages of a book
like wings closed tight.

Look – a bright present
of freshly dyed robes
like folded flames.

*Angi Svarti*

## Nothing That Lives Is Ever Lost
### (for Festival of All Souls)

Nothing that lives is ever lost.
Nor does it become a thing
So ordinary as a ghost.

But quietly, mysteriously
as silent snowfalls in the blue of night,
Life leaves
To live again inside God's shining light.

And when All Hallows comes
We celebrate this holiness, this heaven –
Filled with bright singing
Luminous as flames.

Nothing that lives is ever lost
And in his brightness
God knows all our names.

*Jan Dean*


# Elegy for Bonfire Night

It's over now. The last rocket's
pierced the darkness with its parasol's point of light.

Bangers have stopped banging. Jumping jacks
have stopped jump-jump-jumping.

Roman candles were scarlet, green and blue.
Now they're dark spaces on grass.

Sparklers' circles in cold air
are memories. Soon they'll be dreams.

The Catherine wheel's spun itself out.
It's pinned to the fence, like an ammonite.

Guy's dead on his bonfire, a pitiful sight.
Grown-up voices fade at the garden gate.

I surround my cocoa mug with my hands, trudge up to
   bed.
Write my elegy for bonfire night.

*Fred Sedgwick*


# *Ramadan*

The moon that once was full, ripe and golden,
Wasted away, thin as the rind of a melon,
Like those poor whom sudden ill fortune
Has wasted away like a waning moon.

Like the generous who leave behind
All that was selfish and unkind,
The moon comes out of the tent of the night
And finds its way with a lamp of light.

The lamp of the moon is relit
And the hungry and thirsty
In the desert or the city
Make a feast to welcome it.

*Stanley Cook*

## Eid Mubarak!

Maghrib is the name of the dusk
After the sun goes down
And Safuran is the child in the garden
Watching for the new moon.

It's here! The moon's come! It's Eid!
Eid *Mubarak*! she calls.

Her shalwar-kameez is like poppies
Her dupatta scarf drifts like a breeze
Her bangles gleam as she dances
Eid *Mubarak*! she says.

Her family take gifts to the mosque
Today let no one be sad
Let no one be left out of the feasting
Eid *Mubarak*! instead.

At home there are cards and presents
And smells of spices and sweets
And the women rush to get ready
The great Eid feast.

Dad reminds them that under the stars
Of Africa, Pakistan, India,
Bangladesh
This is the day of happiness.
And under
The stars of England, Safuran says,
Watching her moon. Praise
Be to Allah, Dad says. Praise Him.
And eat!

Bismillahir Rahmanir Rahim.
Eid *Mubarak*!
Happy Eid!

*Berlie Doherty*

## Eid Mubarak!

Eid *Mubarak*! Let's celebrate
the end of the month of fasting.
Eid is a gift to all who wait
in patience for Allah's blessing.

Eid *Mubarak*! We greet neighbours
and share a happy feast with friends.
All are our brothers and sisters.
Praise Allah for the joys He sends.

Eid *Mubarak*! Let's celebrate
the end of the month of fasting.
Wear new clothes on this joyous date
and pray for peace everlasting.

*Debjani Chatterjee*

# Diwali

The dark streets shine,
A dazzling festival of light,
The dark streets shine,
Like necklaces of rich design,
Strings of colours, jewel bright,
A song of stars for our delight,
The dark streets shine.

*June Crebbin*

# Diwali

Diwali lamps are twinkling, twinkling
In the sky and in our homes and hearts.
We welcome all with cheery greetings
And sweets and patterned *rangoli* art.
Lakshmi flies upon her owl tonight;
Incense curls, our future's sparkling bright.

*Debjani Chatterjee*

## Rainbow Rice

When Arzana came to school today
She wore silky robes
That smelled of spices
And excitement.

She spoke of candle flames
And fireworks
That still sparkled in her eyes,
And she brought us bowls
Of rainbow-coloured rice
Tasting of sugar
And sweet surprises.

I shall forget the dates
Of kings and queens
And far-off battles.
I shall forget the names
Of tiny islands
In shimmering seas.
A thousand facts will slip from my mind
Like scuttling mice,

But years from now,
When I am no longer young
The tingle of Arzana's rainbow rice
Will always be
On the tip of my tongue.

*Clare Bevan*

## Prayer for Diwali

O Lord, lead me
from darkness to light, and
from death to immortality.
Let there be peace, peace and real peace.

*Anon.*

## Prince Rama Comes to Longsight

A hundred points of flame
Fleet and weave upon their wicks
On a wet Manchester morning;
But the hall curtains are closed
Against the littered streets,
And incense burns
In a blob of Plasticine
On every window ledge.

The children are changed;
An exotic orient breath
Has lifted their spirits.
No longer poor and grubby kids
From the wrong side of town:
Sayed, from class three,
Is now Prince Rama,

74

Splendid in his cardboard crown,
With Nilam-Sita
Trembling by his side,
And Hanuman, the monkey-king,
Fit to burst with monkey-pride.

Will they forget their words?
Will the infants wail
At first sight of the monster
And its glittering teeth?
No matter.
The legend holds us in its spell,
As in a perfumed bubble,
Lit by lapping flames.

The story moves to its close,
And Miss asks little David
To please stop picking his nose.
She thanks us for our work
And says that next week,
Class Four will give
A Chinese assembly.

The candles are snuffed,
Leaving a greasy smell
To mingle with the boiling cabbage.
Sir nips the incense out.
We are back in rainy Manchester,
But we are not the same.
Though Sayed is himself again.

Puzzling over
Rainbow Maths – Book Three.
And Nilam-Sita has been sent
To fetch a teacher's cup of tea;
Something of Prince Rama
Stays with us;
Sita's beauty,
Hanuman's guile;
Some touch of splendour
From a fabled land.

*John Cunliffe*


## Guru Nanak's Birthday

Candles gleam like cat's eyes
in dark doorways and dusty windows.

Down the street they follow the float
Carrying the Guru Granth Sahib;

Singing hymns;
The crowd proud in their new clothes.

*Anon.*

## *Hanukkah*

Summoning the
 sun

the Hanukkah lamp
 glows

the miracle
 reborn

*David Shalem*

## *Light the Festive Candles*
### *(for Hanukkah)*

Light the first of eight tonight –
the farthest candle to the right.

Light the first and second, too,
when tomorrow's day is through.

Then light three, and then light four –
every dusk one candle more

Till all eight burn bright and high,
honouring a day gone by

When the Temple was restored,
rescued from the Syrian lord,

And an eight-day feast proclaimed –
The Festival of Lights – well named

To celebrate the joyous day
when we regained the right to pray
to our one God in our own way.

*Aileen Fisher*

## You Are the One

'It's Christmas,' the reverend sister had said,
'When Jesus Christ was born.'
And a wide-eyed Hindu girl had dreamed of:
*Somewhere in a manger, angels singing;*
*Three kings, frankincense and myrrh;*
*A lone star rising; lambs bleating from*
*here and there; a donkey quietly watching –*
*Some shepherds kneeling down; a woman in*
*blue and one chuckling baby . . .*

Now I look back and see you clothed in the
sun, moon and stars – What shall I call you?
Shall I call you Jesus? Shall I call you Krishna?
Whatever I call you, I know – You are the
One who holds my hand, when I am lost;
You are the One who chuckles golden light
into my dreams; You are the One who scents
my thoughts with frankincense and myrrh;
You are the One who keeps me smiling
through my tears . . .

*Usha Kishore*

# All of Us Knocking on the Stable Door

Three great kings, three wise men
Tramp across the desert to Bethlehem
Arrive at the inn, don't travel no more
they start knocking at the stable door.

Knocking at the door, knocking at the door
All of us are knocking at the stable door.

I've got myrrh, he's got gold
He's got frankincense and all of us are cold
We stand here shivering, chilled to the core
We're just knocking on the stable door.

The star above it glows in the sky
Burning up the darkness and we know why
A baby king's asleep in the straw
So we start knocking on the stable door.

Travelled some distance, we've travelled far
Melchior, Caspar and Balthazar
We are so wealthy, the baby's so poor
But here we are knocking on the stable door.

Now is the time, now is the hour
To feel the glory, worship the power
We quietly enter, kneel on the floor
Just the other side of the stable door.

Knocking on the door, knocking on the door
All of us knocking at the stable door.

Knocking on the door, knocking on the door
We're all knocking on the stable door.

*David Harmer*

## Listen

Listen.
Far away, the snort of a camel,
The swish of boots in the endless sand,

The whisper of silk and the clatter of ceremonial swords,
Far away.

Listen.
Not so far, the slam of a castle door,
A cry of rage on the midnight air,
A jangle of spurs and the cold thrust of a soldier's
    command,
Not so far.

Listen.
 Closer now, the homely bleat of a ewe among the grasses,
The answering call of her lamb, fresh born,
The rattle of stones on a hillside path,
Closer now.

Listen.
Closer still, the murmur of women in the dark,
The kindly creak of a stable door,
The steady breathing of the sleepy beasts,
Closer still.

Listen.
So close you are almost there,
The singing of the stars,
The soundless flurry of wings,
The soft whimper of a child among the straw,
So close you are almost there.

*Clare Bevan*

# A Christmas Meditation
## (Prayer)

From the old – bring the new
From the past – bring the future
From this place – lead us onward
Touch us with your presence, Lord

*While shepherds watched their flocks by night . . .*
Familiar words, familiar story,
Help us not to take it all for granted
Help us to see you again, as if for the first time
Open up our eyes . . .

From the old – bring the new
From the past – bring the future
From this place – lead us onward
Touch us with your presence, Lord

*The angel of the Lord came down . . .*
The old, old story, seemingly the same every year
Help us not to be complacent
Teach us something fresh
Fill us once again
Open up our eyes . . .

From the old – bring the new
From the past – bring the future
From this place – lead us onward
Touch us with your presence, Lord

*Glory shone around . . .*
Help us to see your glory
In the ordinary everyday birth
In an ordinary everyday stable
In our ordinary everydays
Open up our eyes . . .

From the old – bring the new
From the past – bring the future
From this place – lead us onward
Touch us with your presence, Lord

*Glory to God in the highest . . .*
An imperfect beginning for the beginning of perfection
   on earth
Perfection became flesh and bone in a manger
And your glory came down from on high
So that we might have life
And have it more abundantly
Open up our eyes . . .

From the old – bring the new
From the past – bring the future
From this place – lead us onward
Touch us with your presence, Lord

*And on earth, peace to men . . .*
We pray not only for peace
But for a true understanding of peace
Peace in our own lives, peace in our homes,

Peace in our churches, peace in our town,
Peace in our country, peace in our world,
Peace in our hearts, your peace
Your peace that demands our response
Your peace that demands our action
Your peace that passes all understanding
Open up our eyes . . .

From the old – bring the new
From the past – bring the future
From this place – lead us onwards
Touch us with your presence, Lord

*Paul Cookson*

## from *The Gift*

A star was nestled in the cushions of darkness above the
stable.
The star was watching over the sleepy city of Bethlehem.
And then in the light of the pearly white star
in a stable in David's city,
Jesus Christ was born.

The sun's bare skull sank rapidly into the hills of red
clouds.
The fires danced orange,
Etched deeply against a sky of crimson.

84

The sheep stirred restlessly.
Gold light drained from the air
and it became bleak.
A cold breeze shivered the grass.

A swift noise like gunshot came from the wind
and went to the mountains.
Blinding light filled the sky
and rumbled like thunder.
Lightning flashed.
The shepherds shielded their eyes,
They could not move for fear,
But the light seemed to radiate beauty and gladness.
A hole of glory appeared
In the centre of the abyss.
The light gathered into a knot of brassy hotness
And exploded into shards of ice.
A tall figure emerged slowly
from the fluorescent light.
A clear voice like running water
flew on the air to the ears of the shepherds.

'Do not fear for I am a messenger of God.'

Silence grew
And the smallest of noises
Sounded like rolls of thunder . . .

*Class M, Stone-with-Woodford Primary School*

# Three Kings Never to Be Forgotten

One bright evening
The sky was freckled with stars,
Three wise kings, mounted on great white Stallions
Ride across the dumb desert sand
In search of the newborn King,
Galloping with the wind,
Cantering with the breeze
Pursuing a poet's star.
A village in the distance, no sign of a palace.
Riding on, people stare and wonder
The royal splendour of Balthazar's
Heavy, woven cloth.
The dazzle of Caspar's sunshine draping cloak,
Melchior's astonishing fiery shimmering shawl,
Speckled with stars.
Colours dance in the atmosphere
As cloaks leap and flirt across the kings' backs.

Almost there.
Almost there.

An old battered stable, alive with joy.
People crowd round, 'Make way for the kings!'
A baby cries, clothed in white.
A gentle mother tenderly rocks her prince.
A proud father stands aside.
Cloaks silently brush against each other.

The Holy one at last.
Gifts glitter and gleam, before the baby.
A new Mystery is born.

*Poppy Corbett, aged 10*

## from *The Gift*

As a fisherman uses his rod.

As a shepherd uses his crook.

Jesus used his heart to lead

and light the minds of men.

*Class M, Stone-with-Woodford*
*Primary School*

## Christmas Morning

Last year
On Christmas morning
We got up really early
And took the dog for a walk
Across the downs

It wasn't snowing
But the hills were white with frost
And our breath froze
In the air

Judy rushed around like a crazy thing
As though Christmas
meant something special to her

The sheep huddled together
looking tired
as if they'd been up all night
watching the stars

We stood at the highest point
And thought about what Christmas means
And looked over the white hills
And looked up at the blue sky

And the hills seemed
To go on forever
And the sky had no bounds
And you could imagine
A world at peace

*Roger Stevens*

# Remembering Snow

I did not sleep last night.
The falling snow was beautiful and white.
I went downstairs,
And opened wide the door.
I had not seen such snow before.
Our grubby little street had gone –
All looked brand new, and everywhere
There was a pureness in the air.
I felt such peace. Watching every flake
I felt more and more awake.
I thought I'd learned all there was to know
About the trillion million different kinds
Of swirling frosty flakes of falling snow.
But that was not so.
I did not know how vividly it lit
The world with such a peaceful glow.
Upstairs my parents slept.
I could not drag myself away from that sight
To call them down and have them share
The mute miracle of the snow.
It seemed to fall for me alone.
How beautiful our little street had grown!

*Brian Patten*

## Shine Out, Fair Sun

Shine out, fair sun, with all your heat,
Show all your thousand-coloured light!
Black Winter freezes to his sea;
The grey wolf howls he does so bite;
Crookt Age on three knees creeps the street;
The boneless fish close quaking lies
And eats for cold his aching feet;
The stars in icicles arise:
Shine out, and make this winter night
Our beauty's Spring, our Prince of light.

*Anon.*

## Winter, Goodbye

Goodbye, Winter.
Adios, snow and ice.
Farewell, roaring fires
And wine laced with spice.

Goodbye, frozen fingers.
Goodbye, frozen earth.
Welcome, hints of plenty.
Au revoir, dearth.

Branches now are budding.
Crocuses are up.
Daffodil and snowdrop,
Daisy and buttercup.

Birds have started nesting.
The garden wall is mossed.
Get going, Winter,
And take your frost.

Take your frost with you.
Get on your way.
We welcomed you a while.
But not today!

It's time you were going.
Your job is done.
Dandelions are lifting
Their heads to the sun.

The year is rested now.
Can't you feel the itch?
There's blossom on the trees,
Spawn in the ditch.

Winter, goodbye.
It's March now. Remember?
Hit the road, old friend.
See you in December.

*Gerard Benson*

## On New Year's Eve

Wise as an owl the old year blinks
And silent into shadows sinks.

A secret bud the new year waits
And beckons from beyond the gates.

His memories packed, the traveller stands
And steps in hope across the sands.

*John Foster*

## Ten New Year's Resolutions

To do my homework every night / if there's no match on TV

To be nice to Miss Tomkins / ugh!

To visit Gran / on her baking day

To save some pocket money / to spend on ice cream

To bring my sports kit back
for Mum to wash / before it walks home

To tidy my room / ~~at weekends~~ occasionally

To go to bed on time / with a torch

To eat at least *one* green vegetable / a pea

To improve my maths / a fraction

To scrap these resolutions / without hesitation

*Mina Johnson*

# Song for a Birthday
### (to be said with the appropriate name in the gaps)

Is it raining outside? Is it snowing?
Is the sun shining bright in the sky?
Is it foggy or grey? Is today a bright day?
It's a very good day. This is why,

Well,

Today is - - - - - - -'s birthday
And everyone gathers to say
'Today is - - - - - - -'s birthday,
- - - - - -'s own special day.'

Is it pizza for lunch? Or spaghetti?
Is it chips? Is it cheese? Is it beans?
Is it curry and rice (yes, that would be nice)?
It's - - - - - - -'s day, and that means

That

Today is - - - - - - -'s birthday
And everyone gathers to say
'Today is - - - - - - -'s birthday,
- - - - - - -'s own special day.'

Is it maths? Is it English, or Music?
Is it History? Science? PE?
It's – – – – – –'s day, it's a simply great day,
For her*, and for you, and for me

Cos

Today is - - - - - - -'s birthday
And everyone gathers to say
'Today is - - - - - - -'s birthday,
- - - - - - -'s own special day.'

*Fred Sedgwick*

*or him, of course

# *Possible Presents*

The lick of a tall ice cream
and the first burnt nose of summer.

The jumper which shrunk in the wash
back to its usual size.

A bowl of red tulips
which curl up their petals at night.

A camouflaged frog jumping
between caramel leaves.

Bread baked this morning
spread with Somerset butter.

The blackbird which sings in the tree
each day at a quarter to four.

*Chrissie Gittins*

# Wedding Day

Lillian McEever is bride for the day
Wearing Mummy's old wedding dress long locked away
And a posy of dandelions for her bouquet
And a tiara of daisies.

Birdsong showers silver on Institute Drive
Where Lillian waits for her guests to arrive
And the shouts and the laughter shake the morning alive
There's a wedding today.

Past the brook they wind where the cherry trees bloom
Casting white showers of blossom over bride and groom
And grandmothers dream in curtained front rooms
And remember.

Lillian McEever, forget not this day
For spring mornings die but memories stay
When the past like the dress is long locked away
And the leaves fall.

*Gareth Owen*

## Mehndi Time
*To welcome Tulika to our family*

The love of family and friends –
at *mehndi** time, at *mehndi* time –
the joy of stories and laughter –
at *mehndi* time, at *mehndi* time,
embrace me like a magic ring
as they clap their hands and sing:

> *May the new bride bring a blessing,*
> mehndi *magic mark her wedding.*
> *With designs – intricate and neat –*
> *we'll decorate her hands and feet.*

With bright lines of ochre colour –
at *mehndi* time, at *mehndi* time –
my sisters pattern loving warmth –
at *mehndi* time, at *mehndi* time.
In life my journey may be far
as I pursue my *mehndi* star.

> *Painted shells and lotus flowers*
> *decorate these happy hours.*
> *Rich mango leaves and tree of life –*
> *love's anchors for our new-wed wife.*

I will nourish tradition's fruit
at *mehndi* time, at *mehndi* time.
What memories I will cherish –
at *mehndi* time, of *mehndi* time!
Like *mehndi* bushes, cool and green,
may *mehndi* make my life serene.

> *Her feet are tinted coral-rose,*
> *her hands are jewels in repose.*
> *May her new life flow with blessing,*
> mehndi *magic mark her wedding.*

It's *mehndi* time, it's *mehndi* time . . .

*Debjani Chatterjee*

\**Mehndi*: henna

# Extract from the *Book of Ecclesiastes*

To every thing there is a season,
　and a time to every purpose under heaven:
A time to be born, and a time to die;
　a time to plant, and a time to pluck up that which is
　　planted;
A time to kill, and a time to heal;
a time to break down, and a time to build up;
A time to weep, and a time to laugh;
　a time to mourn, and a time to dance;

A time to cast away stones, and a time to gather stones
together;
a time to embrace, and a time to refrain from embracing;
A time to get, and a time to lose;
a time to keep, and a time to cast away;
A time to rend, and a time to sew;
a time to keep silence, and a time to speak;
A time to love, and a time to hate;
a time of war, and a time of peace.

*King James Bible*

# Thoughts, Feelings and Faith

# ANGER

## *When I Was Angry*

When I was angry
I screamed at my mummy.

Then I was quiet
for a long long time.

I curled up
in her arms

and said 'Sorry'
and she said

'That's all right
My Little Chickadee'

and then she tickled me.

*Fred Sedgwick*

# ABILITIES

## *These Are the Hands*

These are the hands that wave
These are the hands that clap
These are the hands that pray
These are the hands that tap

These are the hands that grip
These are the hands that write
These are the hands that paint
These are the hands that fight

These are the hands that hug
These are the hands that squeeze
These are the hands that point
These are the hands that tease

These are the hands that fix
These are the hands that mend
These are the hands that give
These are the hands that lend

These are the hands that take
These are the hands that poke
These are the hands that heal
These are the hands that stroke

These are the hands that hold
These are the hands that love
These are the hands of mine
That fit me like a glove

*Paul Cookson*

# BEING THOUGHTFUL

## *Actions Speak*

He never said a word, my brother.
Just brought me a tissue – or two –
a cup of tea, chocolate biscuits
and his copy of the *Beano*.

Left them on my bedside table,
squeezed my shoulder, smiled
and left me alone for a while.

Never said a word.
Never had to.
Knew just how I felt.

*Paul Cookson*

# BEING YOURSELF

## *Sometimes*

Sometimes I don't like myself
but then sometimes I do,
and sometimes it's so hard to know
if what I feel is true.

Like when I have a tantrum,
is that all people see?
I'm only like that sometimes,
that fury's not all me.

Sometimes, I go racing through
the playground in my head
which is awkward if I should
be doing geography instead.

Those sometimes I go missing
whilst physically still here,
they're much the best of sometimes
that's when I disappear.

For then I go all over
from Ecuador to Mars,
to nesting with the eagle
and swapping round the stars.

That magic sometimes when I feel
beyond the moon and free,
the sometimes I forget myself
and let myself be me.

*Stewart Henderson*

# BELIEF/FAITH

## *A Faithless Creed*

I believe in Australia
but have never been there.
I believe in Barnsley FC
but don't pay to see them play.
I believe in university education
but to what degree?
I believe in lions
but not to hang around with.
I believe in outer space
but have no plans to visit.
I believe in Sky tv
but am not a subscriber.
I believe in many things
but is that the same
as having faith?
A faith that makes a difference
to my daily
living
doing
and being.
A faith that is something firm
beneath my feet.
What do you believe?

*Tony Bower*

# BLESSING

## *Benediction*

Thanks to the ear
that someone may hear

Thanks to seeing
that someone may see

Thanks to feeling
that someone may feel

Thanks to touch
that one may be touched

Thanks to flowering of white moon
and spreading shawl of black night
holding villages and cities together

*James Berry*

## *May You Always*

May your smile be ever present
May your skies be always blue
May your path be ever onward
May your heart be ever true

May your dreams be full to bursting
May your steps be always sure
May the fire within your soul
Blaze on for evermore

May you live to meet ambition
May you strive to pass each test
May you find the love your life deserves
May you always have the best

May your happiness be plentiful
May your regrets be few
May you always be my best friend
May you always . . . just be you

*Paul Cookson*

# BOASTING

## *The Cheer-up Song*

No one likes a boaster
And I'm not one to boast,
But everyone who knows me knows
That I'm the most.

I'm the most attractive, I'm
The Media Superstar,
One hundred per cent in-tell-i-gent
And pop-u-lar.

All my jokes are funny.
Every one's a laugh.
Madonna pays me money for
My au-to-graph.

For I'm the snake's pyjamas, I'm
The bumble-bee's patella,
I'm a juicesome peach at a picnic on the beach, I'm
The rainmaker's umbrella.

Yes I'm the death-by-chocolate, I'm
The curried beans on toast,
And everyone who knows me knows that
I'm the most.

Tee-rr-eye-double-eff-eye-see
Triffic! TRIFFIC! TRIFFIC!
Yes it's me! ME! MEEE!

*John Whitworth*

# BULLYING

## *The Bully*

I'm the big bully,
The one they all fear,
So you'd better watch out
Whenever I'm near.

I look for the weak kids,
The ones who feel shy,
And my one aim in life
Is to force them to cry.

I look for the small kids
Who tremble and run,
I chase them and hit them,
That's my kind of fun.

I look for the good kids
Enjoying their games,
But they don't laugh for long
When *I* call them names.

I look for the bright kids,
I hate teachers' pets,
And if I should catch one
You know what he gets.

When I'm in the playground
They all back away,
They're scared of my temper
And what I might say.

The big kids walk past me
But none of them stay,
I'm not really bothered,
I don't want to play.

So I stand by myself
Just kicking the wall
And no one comes near me,
No one at all . . .

*Clare Bevan*


## Bully

I play with a ball.
They take the ball and say,
'Who said you could play with a ball?'

I walk away.
They chase me and say,
'Who said you could walk away?'

I hide.
They find me and say,
'Who said you could hide?'

I cry.
They say,
'What are you crying about?'

*John Coldwell*


# Agreement

He was bigger than me
So I had to agree,
Before being hurt,
That I was a squirt,
My haircut was trashy,
My spectacles flashy,
My dad was a failure,
My mum loved a sailor,
My favourite group couldn't sing,
The team I supported couldn't win a thing
And the trainers I'd got were not fit to be worn
And the world would better a better place if I had not been
    born.
He was bigger than me
So I had to agree.

*John Coldwell*

111

# COPING WITH ANGER

## *What to Do When Angry*

Breathe slowly,
Count to ten.
Run upstairs
And down again.
Think of birthdays,
Stroke your pet.
Don't say something
You'll regret!

*Sue Cowling*

## *Let It Go*

When you go off
to sleep at night
if you can feel
the fire so bright

Don't give it air
don't let it grow
or cloud your mind
or burn your soul

Don't let it stay
don't give it light
just cast it out
into the night

Before you dream
it must be so:
just let that fire
go

*James Carter*

# COPING WITH BEING HURT

## *The Hurt Boy and the Birds*

The hurt boy talked to the birds
and fed them the crumbs of his heart.

It was not easy to find the words
for secrets he hid under his skin.
The hurt boy spoke of a bully's fist
that made his face a bruised moon –
his spectacles stamped to ruin.

It was not easy to find the words
for things that nightly hissed
as if his pillow was a hideaway for creepy-crawlies –
the note sent to the girl he fancied
held high in mockery.

But the hurt boy talked to the birds
and their feathers gave him welcome –

Their wings taught him new ways to become.

*John Agard*

# COPING WITH HARSH WORDS

## *Night Puzzle*

I sleep with those words
going round and round
my head and why did
you say those words
you said and how can
I sleep with those words . . .

*Roger Stevens*

# DREAMS

## *Let No One Steal Your Dreams*

Let no one steal your dreams
Let no one tear apart
The burning of ambition
That fires the drive inside your heart

Let no one steal your dreams
Let no one tell you that you can't
Let no one hold you back
Let no one tell you that you won't

Set your sights and keep them fixed
Set your sights on high
Let no one steal your dreams
Your only limit is the sky

Let no one steal your dreams
Follow your heart
Follow your soul
For only when you follow them
Will you feel truly whole

Set your sights and keep them fixed
Set your sights on high
Let no one steal your dreams
Your only limit is the sky

*Paul Cookson*

## Hold Fast
### *(a rondelet)*

Hold fast the dream
within the chaos of the day.
Hold fast the dream
while dancing to the bright lights' beam
along your shadow-scattered way.
Just pause awhile and softly say:
'Hold fast the dream.'

*Brian D'Arcy*

## Wings

If I had wings
I would touch the fingertips of clouds
and glide on the wind's breath.

If I had wings
I would taste a chunk of the sun
as hot as peppered curry.

If I had wings
I would listen to the clouds of sheep bleat
that graze on the blue.

If I had wings
    I would breathe deep and sniff
        the scent of raindrops.

If I had wings
    I would gaze at the people
        who cling to the earth's crust.

If I had wings
    I would dream of
        swimming the deserts
            and walking the seas.

*Pie Corbett*

# FEAR

## *Big Fears*

Twenty-five feet above Sian's house
hangs a thick wire cable
that droops and sags between
two electricity pylons.

A notice says it carries 320,000 volts
from one metallic scarecrow to the next,
then on to the next and the next
right across the countryside to the city.

The cable sways above Sian's council house
making her radio crackle and sometimes
making her television go on the blink.

If it's a very windy night
Sian gets frightened because
she thinks the cable might snap,
fall on to the roof and electrocute
everyone as they sleep.

This is Sian's Big Fear.

Outside Matthew's bedroom there
is a tall tree – taller than the house.
In summer it is heavy with huge leaves.
In winter it stands lonely as a morning moon.

On a windy night Matthew worries
that the tree might be blown down
and crash through his bedroom window.
It would certainly kill him and his cat
If it was sleeping under the bed
where it usually goes.

This is Matthew's Big Fear.

Outside Karen's bedroom there's nothing
but a pleasant view: meadows, hedges, sheep
and some distant gentle hills.
There's nothing sinister, nothing to worry about.

But at night, in the dark, Karen thinks
the darting shapes on the ceiling
are really the shadows of a ghost's
great cold hands and that the night noises
made by the water pipes are
the screeches and groans of attic skeletons.

*John Rice*

## The Dark

Why are we so afraid of the dark?
It doesn't bite and doesn't bark
or chase old ladies round the park
or steal your sweeties for a lark

And though it might not let you see
it lets you have some privacy
and gives you time to go to sleep –
provides a place to hide or weep

It cannot help but be around
when beastly things make beastly sounds
or back doors slam and windows creak
or cats have fights and voices shriek

The dark is cosy, still and calm
and never does you any harm
in the loft, below the sink
it's somewhere nice and quiet to think

Deep in cupboards, pockets too
it's always lurking out of view
why won't it come out till it's night?
Perhaps the dark's afraid of light

*James Carter*

## Don't Be Scared

The dark is only a blanket
for the moon to put on her bed.

The dark is a private cinema
for the movie dreams in your head.

The dark is a little black dress
to show off the sequin stars.

The dark is the wooden hole
behind the strings of happy guitars.

The dark is a jeweller's velvet cloth
where children sleep like pearls.

The dark is a spool of film
to photograph boys and girls,

so smile in your sleep in the dark.
Don't be scared.

*Carol Ann Duffy*

# Words
### to all the staff at PSAC, Pulrose, Isle of Man

I am enveloped by the darkness of silence,
I am lost, frightened and all alone –
My prayer has no words, My Lord!
Take my tears for prayer,
take my sighs for prayer,
take my heartbeat for prayer
and give me the light of words . . .

*Find me in the peal of temple bells,*
*find me in the light of oil lamps,*
*find me in the fragrance of incense*
*and I shall be the words of your prayer . . .*

*Usha Kishore*

# FEELING SAFE

## *Safe*

Safe where I cannot die yet,
  Safe where I hope to lie too.
Safe from the fume and fret
  You, and you,
Whom I never forget.

Safe from the frost and snow
  Safe from the storm and the sun
Safe where the seeds wait to grow
  One by one
And to come back in blow.

*Christina Rossetti*

# GIVING THANKS

## *I Thank You, Lord*
### *(Muslim prayer)*

I thank you, Lord, for knowing me
  better than I know myself,
And for letting me know myself
  better than others know me.

Make me, I ask you then,
   better than others know me.
Make me, I ask you then,
   better than they suppose,
And forgive me for what they do not know.

*Anon.*

## Thank You

Thank you for the blanket
that spreads on my bed
Thank you for the pillow
that cradles my head
Thank you for the darkness
that rolls through the skies
Thank you for the tiredness
that closes my eyes.

Thank you for the windows
that keep out the storm
Thank you for the heating
that helps me stay warm
Thank you for the four walls
that make up my room
Thank you for the cold light
that falls from the moon.

Thank you for the loved ones
who sleep in this place
Thank you for the memories
that light up my face
Thank you for the silence
that comes with the night
Thank you for the feeling
that everything's right.

*Steve Turner*

# GUILT

## *Blushing*

When Mr Wheeler
Announced in assembly
That someone had been stealing

I always had this terrible feeling
That I'd be the one to blush –
A sudden flush of guilt,
Even though I wasn't to blame.

Deep inside me
There must have been a hidden shame
That would rise up
To break surface
In a full frontal rush of red.

I'd think to myself –
'Whatever you do,
Don't blush'.

But Mr Wheeler
Scanned the rows of children
Eyes like searchlights
Seeking out enemy planes
Till he'd catch me
With his telescopic sights

Blushing with innocence.

*Pie Corbett*

# HAPPINESS

## *Happy Poem*

Happy as a rainbow
happy as a bee
happy as a dolphin
splashing in the sea

Happy as bare feet
running on the beach
happy as a sunflower
happy as a peach

Happy as a poppy
happy as a spoon
dripping with honey
happy as June

Happy as a banjo
plucking on a tune
happy as a Sunday
lazy afternoon

Happy as a memory
shared by two
happy as me . . .
when I'm with you!

*James Carter*

## What's My Name?

I'm the sun that lights the playground before the day
  begins
I'm the smiles when teacher cracks a joke. I'm the giggles
  and the grins.
In assembly I'm the trophy that the winning team collects
In your maths book I'm the page of sums where every
  one's correct
I'm the pure blue sky and leafy green that wins the prize in
  art

I'm steamy, creamy custard dribbling down the cook's jam
    tart
I'm the act of kindness when you lent your kit to Mia
I'm the noise of playtime rising through the stratosphere
I'm the star you were awarded for your startling poetry
I'm the school gates swinging open on the stroke of half
    past three
If you look for me, you'll find me. What's my name? Can
    you guess?
I live just round the corner and my name is . . . ?

*Roger Stevens*

# HOPE

## *Hopes*

Some days my hopes
Are made of glass, of light, of ice
So fragile that they almost crack.

I'm afraid my hopes will slip
Right through my fingers
Shattering into a thousand pieces.

But they never do.

Other days my hopes are heavy
A big, buckled bag on my back
So full of stones, my shoulders ache.

I'm afraid my hopes will crash
Down to the ground
Spill and tumble into the gutter.

But they never do.

Hold on to your hopes with both hands
Fragile or heavy, light or a burden
Never let them go.

*David Harmer*

## Things with Feathers

*'"Hope" is the thing with feathers*
*That perches in the soul'* –
*Emily Dickinson*

Give us a tune, thing with feathers –
sing it in all weathers.

Sing it for eagle, osprey, wren,
kite, owl, moorhen,

and all those feathered others –
cousins, sisters, brothers –

who share with us here
our precarious atmosphere,

128

beating its thinness till it rings
with their songs and wings.

Sing for each threatened kind
that's nested here time out of mind –

sing for the sapphire blur
of the kingfisher,

for the thrush who once lorded it
on our chestnut summit,

for the fewer sparrows brawling
under eaves and awnings,

for the bullfinch with the furnace
of chest who's forsaken us,

for the grebe with the fish-hook
in its half-shut beak,

for fading lapwing and lark,
and silenced corncrake.

Sing against birdsong's
sad diminishing.

Let that be your tune,
thing with feathers.

Sing it in all weathers.

*Robert Hull*

## *Hope*

Hope is the thing with feathers
That perches in the soul,
And sings the tune without the words,
And never stops at all,

And sweetest in the gale is heard;
And sore must be the storm
That could abash the little bird
That kept so many warm.

I've heard it in the chillest land,
And on the strangest sea;
Yet, never, in extremity,
It asked a crumb of me.

*Emily Dickinson*

# IDENTITY

## *What's Your Colour?*

What's your colour, the colour of your skin,
The colour of the envelope that you're wrapped in?

Is it like chocolate, tea or coffee?
Is it like marzipan, fudge or toffee?
Peaches and cream or a strawberry milkshake
Or does it look more like a curranty cake?

What's your colour, the colour of your skin,
The colour of the envelope that you're wrapped in?

Are you a map of your past disasters?
Grazes and scratches and sticking plasters?
Bites from mosquitoes, a yellow-blue bruise
And a couple of blisters from rather tight shoes?

What's your colour, the colour of your skin,
The colour of the envelope that you're wrapped in?

How does it go when the weather's sunny?
Brown as a berry or gold as honey?
Does it go freckly or peeling and sore?
Is there a mark from the watch that you wore?

What's your colour, the colour of your skin,
The colour of the envelope that you're wrapped in?

Do you go pink when you're all embarrassed?
Sweaty and red when you're hot and harassed?
Bumpy and blue on a cold winter's day?
When it's time for your bath are you usually grey?

What's your colour, the colour of your skin,
The colour of the envelope that you're wrapped in?

*Julia Donaldson*

# IMAGINATION

## *Inside My Head*

Inside my head there's a forest,
A castle, a cottage, a king,
A rose, a thorn, some golden hair,
A turret, a tower, a ring.

A horse, a prince, a secret word,
A giant, a gaol, a pond,
A witch, a snake, a bubbling pot,
A wizard, a warlock, a wand.

Inside my head there's an ocean,
A parrot, a pirate, a gull,
A cave, a sword, a silver coin,
A princess, an island, a skull.

A ghost, a ghoul, a creaking stair,
A shadow, a shudder, a shout,
A flame, a grave, a swirling mist,
A rainbow, an angel, a cloud.

Inside my head there's a country
Of mountains and valleys and streams,
It all comes alive when I listen
To stories, to poems, to dreams.

*Steve Turner*

# INCLUSION

## *Inclusion*

Standing in the spotlight
Listening to the crowd go wild
I'm only in Year 8
But one of the stars of the Christmas plays

I'm at the top of the climbing wall
I'm the king of 'Alton Castle'
I've overcome my fear
The view's amazing from here

I got to bleat as a sheep
In Peter Rose's play
Running around the stage,
Part of the flock

In the gang
One of the crowds
That's me
Martin Shorter

*Martin Shorter*

## *Inclusion*

Staring at the playground
Children playing in their playground way.
Jumping, hopping, running, jogging
Playing in their playground way

Day by day I watch them in my corner
All alone,
If only they would play with me instead of
Leaving me on my own.
My legs don't work the way yours do
I really want to be like you
But every day I watch them play, all alone on my own.

Playing with the playground
Children playing in their playground way
Jumping, hopping, running, jogging
Playing in their playground way.

They push me round and round and listen to
The squeaky sound
Of my wheels moving the playground ground.
My wish has come true, to be with you.
Now my individuality
Has bought me lots of popularity.

Playing with the playground
Children playing in their playground way
Jumping, hopping, running, jogging
Playing in their playground way.

*Venetia Taylor*

# INDIVIDUALITY

## *Write Your Name*

Write your name
with a stick
in the sand

Write your name
in the snow
with your hand

Write your name
on a board
with a chalk

Write your name
in the air
as you talk

Write your name
as you breathe
on glass

Write your name
with your friends
in class

Write your name
all curly
and small

Write your name
all pointy
and tall

Write your name
in the dark
at night

Write your name
in the sky
with a kite

Write your name,
whatever you do –
write your name
to celebrate
             YOU!

*James Carter*

# One

Only one of me
and nobody can get a second one
from a photocopy machine.

Nobody has the fingerprints I have.
Nobody can cry my tears, or laugh my laugh
or have my expectancy when I wait.

But anybody can mimic my dance with my dog.
Anybody can howl how I sing out of tune.
And mirrors can show me multiplied
many times, say, dressed up in red
or dressed up in grey.

Nobody can get into my clothes for me
or feel my fall for me, or do my running.
Nobody hears my music for me, either.

I am just this one.
Nobody else makes the words
I shape with sound, when I talk.

But anybody can act how I stutter in a rage.
Anybody can copy echoes I make.
And mirrors can show me multiplied
many times, say, dressed up in green
or dressed up in blue.

*James Berry*

# JOY

## *Ayii, Ayii, Ayii*

Ayii, ayii, ayii
My arms, they wave in the air,
My hands, they flutter behind my back
They wave above my head
Like the wings of a bird.
Let me move my feet.
Let me dance.
Let me shrug my shoulders.
Let me shake my body.
Let me crouch down.
My arms, let me fold them.
Let me hold my hands under my chin.

*Traditional Inuit*

## *Just One Wish (feeling full of joy)*

If I had only one wish
I would drop it in a rippling pool
and watch the concentric circles
it would make as it plunged downwards
fragmenting the surface of the water.

If I had only one wish
I'd throw it high into the blue heaven

and watch it as it arched over
and tumbled down, creating
a rainbow of joy in the roof of the world.

If I had only one wish
I'd plant it deep in brown earth
and watch as it pierced the loam
with a pointed spear
and grew into a magnificent tree.

If I had only one wish
I'd burn it like incense
and savour the aroma as it wafted
far away on the winds of perfume
and dissipated on the thermals of life.

If I had only one wish
I should wish that everyone
could once again be filled with childlike joy
So that the magic and beauty of the world
would once again be a daily miracle.

*Janis Priestley*

# LAUGHING

## *Prayer to Laughter*

Oh Laughter
giver of relaxed mouths

you who rule our belly with tickles
you who come when not called
you who can embarrass us at times

send us stitches on our sides
shake us till the water reaches our eyes
buckle our knees till we cannot stand

we whose faces are grim and shattered
we whose hearts are no longer hearty
Oh Laughter we beg you

crack us up
crack us up

*John Agard*

# LONELINESS

## *Playground Haiku*

Everyone says our
playground is overcrowded
but I feel lonely.

*Helen Dunmore*

## *To Be Alone*

To be alone is like being
in a grave alone
in the earth.
Like a
Star floating
in
Space slowly
moving.
To be alone is
like standing
in a dark room holding
a
stick.
To be alone is
like

one word closed inside
a book.
To be alone is
like a soul
of a man hiding in
the trees.

*Matthew Cole, aged 7*

# LOVE

## *Love You More*

Do I love you
to the moon and back?
No I love you
more than that

I love you to the desert sands
the mountains, stars
the planets and

I love you to the deepest sea
and deeper still
through history

Before beyond I love you then
I love you now
I'll love you when

The sun's gone out
the moon's gone home
and all the stars are fully grown

When I no longer say these words
I'll give them to the wind, the birds
so that they will still be heard

I love you

*James Carter*

## Contradictions of Love

As fragile as an eggshell bauble
    On a Christmas tree,
But durable as gleaming steel
    Of knife, or sword, or key.

Sweet as the fragrance of the rose
    Or honey from the bee,
But cold and scentless as the snow,
    And salty as the sea.

As gentle as a summer breeze
    Or mother's lullaby,
But burly as a hurricane
    Or thunder in the sky.

As magical as witches' spells
   Or blackbirds in a pie,
But plain and simple as good bread,
   Without which we would die.

*Vernon Scannell*

# LYING

## *Word of a Lie*

I am the fastest runner in my school and that's
NO WORD OF A LIE
I've got gold fillings in my teeth and that's
NO WORD OF A LIE
In my garden, I've got my own big bull and that's
NO WORD OF A LIE
I'm brilliant at giving my enemies grief and that's
NO WORD OF A LIE
I can multiply three billion and twenty-seven by nine
   billion four thousand and one in two seconds and that's
NO WORD OF A LIE
I can calculate the distance between planets before you've
   had toast and that's
NO WORD OF A LIE
I can always tell when my best pals boast and that's
NO WORD OF A LIE
I'd been round the world twice before I was three and a
   quarter and that's

NO WORD OF A LIE
I am definitely my mother's favourite daughter and that's
NO WORD OF A LIE
I am brilliant at fake laughter, I go Ha aha Ha ha ha and
    that's
NO WORD OF A LIE
I can tell the weather from one look at the sky and that's
NO WORD OF A LIE
I can predict disasters, floods, earthquakes and murders
    and that's
NO WORD OF A LIE
I can always tell when other people lie and that's
NO WORD OF A LIE
I can even tell if someone is going to die and that's
NO WORD OF A LIE
I am the most popular girl in my entire school and that's
NO WORD OF A LIE
I know the golden rule, don't play the fool, don't boast, be
    shy and that's
NO WORD OF A LIE
I am sensitive, I listen, I have kind brown eyes and that's
NO WORD OF A LIE

You don't believe me do you?
ALL RIGHT, ALL RIGHT, ALL RIGHT
I am the biggest liar in my school and that's
NO WORD OF A LIE

*Jackie Kay*

# MEMORIES

## *Memories*

It's hard to forget the past when so much has happened to
  me
Before the illness happened I was full of glee.
I used to be an acrobat and a tap dancer too
Now Eleanor is placing her footsteps in the things I used to
  do.

People look at me differently in my wheelchair
But what they don't know is this
I used to dance and skip and ride my bike
And do so many things I used to like
I still have these memories so sweet
Remember these words when we happen to meet

*K. Clays*

# NAME CALLING

## *It Hurts*

It hurts when someone makes remarks
About the clothes I wear,
About the foods I refuse to eat
Or the way I cover my hair.

It hurts when someone laughs and jokes
About the way I speak.
'Ignore them,' says my dad, but it's hard
To turn the other cheek.

It hurts when someone calls me names
Because of the colour of my skin.
Everyone's different outside,
But we're all the same within.

*John Foster*

# PEACE

## from *His Pilgrimage*

Give me my scallop-shell of quiet,
My staff of faith to walk upon,
My scrip of joy, immortal diet,
My bottle of salvation,
My gown of Glory, hope's true gage;
And thus I'll take my pilgrimage.

*Sir Walter Raleigh*

# *I Wandered Lonely As a Cloud*

I wandered lonely as a cloud
That floats on high o'er vales and hills,
When all at once I saw a crowd,
A host, of golden daffodils;
Beside the lake, beneath the trees,
Fluttering and dancing in the breeze.

Continuous as the stars that shine
And twinkle on the milky way,
They stretched in neverending line
Along the margin of a bay:
Ten thousand saw I at a glance,
Tossing their heads in sprightly dance.

The waves beside them danced; but they
Outdid the sparkling waves in glee:
A poet could not but be gay,
In such a jocund company:
I gazed – and gazed – but little thought
What wealth the show to me had brought:

For oft, when on my couch I lie
In vacant or in pensive mood,
They flash upon that inward eye
Which is the bliss of solitude;
And then my heart with pleasure fills
And dances with the daffodils.

*William Wordsworth*

# *Imagine*

Imagine, there's a heaven above us,
and not merely a blanket of sky.
Imagine, there's a God who cares for us,
more to life than meets the eye.
Imagine, this troubled, shattered earth,
restless and confused,
discovering its real, true worth,
finding that we've been saved,
from a hell without love,
from a life without reason.
Imagine, peace like a dove,
descending for a forever season,
in the heart of mankind,
where the war of the soul is won,
and all that was lost we find,
in the God who has come
into our hearts and our mind,
living with us in the world he created.
Imagine.

*Tony Bower*

# PRIDE

## *Pride Comes Before a Fall*

'Pride comes before a fall,'
My dad used to say
Whenever my little brother
Started showing off.

Now Dad sits on the sofa,
Looking sheepish,
With his leg propped on a stool
And his toes sticking out of the plaster.

Last week,
As he was prancing round the garden,
Pretending he was Paul Gascoigne,
He trod on the ball.
He fell awkwardly
And broke his ankle.

'Don't expect any sympathy from me,'
Said my mum.
'You should know better at your age.'

'Pride comes before a fall,'
Says my brother
On his way out
To play football with his friends.

*John Foster*

# QUARRELLING

## *The Quarrel*

I quarrelled with my brother
I don't know what about,
One thing led to another
And somehow we fell out.
The start of it was slight,
The end of it was strong,
He said he was right,
I knew he was wrong!

We hated one another.
The afternoon turned black.
Then suddenly my brother
Thumped me on the back,
And said, 'Oh, come along!
We can't go on all night –
I was in the wrong.'
So he was in the right.

*Eleanor Farjeon*

## A Poison Tree

I was angry with my friend:
I told my wrath, my wrath did end.
I was angry with my foe:
I told it not, my wrath did grow.

And I watered it in fears,
Night and morning with my tears;
And I sunnèd it with smiles,
And with soft deceitful wiles.

And it grew both day and night,
Till it bore an apple bright;
And my foe beheld it shine,
And he knew that it was mine,

And into my garden stole
When the night had veiled the pole:
In the morning glad I see
My foe outstretched beneath the tree.

*William Blake*

# QUIETNESS

## *Tree Frog Song*

It was the quiet of a whisper,
And the gently spoken word,
That dislodged the sleeping Mr . . . Frog
That's the one he heard.
And no one listens when you shout
They're just being polite to hear you out,
But there really isn't any doubt;
It's a quiet word that stays in your heart.
It's a quiet word that stays in your heart.
It's a quiet word that stays in your heart
When all the noise has gone.

The West wind bellowed and he bawled
And the North wind yelled and called and called
And the East wind roared and roared and roared,
They were all so sure, he'd hit the floor!
But no one listens when you shout
They're just being polite to hear you out,
But there really isn't any doubt;
It's a quiet word that stays in your heart.
It's a quiet word that stays in your heart.
It's a quiet word that stays in your heart
When all the noise has gone.

The South wind whispered gently in his ear,
Have a snooze, Mr Frog my dear!
She rocked his branch just enough,
Then knocked him off with a gentle little puff!
And no one listens when you shout
They're just being polite to hear you out,
But there really isn't any doubt;
It's a quiet word that stays in your heart.
It's a quiet word that stays in your heart.
It's a quiet word that stays in your heart
When all the noise has gone.

*Pete Mountstephen, St Stephens Primary School*

# QUESTIONING

## *Questions*

How? Who can say how?
How did we travel from Then until Now?
Galaxies hurled and hurtled apart –
How in the world did the whole thing start?
Was there a bang? How long ago?
Does anyone anywhere really know?

Why? Who can say why?
Why did the dinosaur dynasty die?
Why should a beast whose power was colossal
Give up the ghost and turn into a fossil?
Give us a clue; why was it so?
Does anyone anywhere really know?

When? Who can say when?
When did our ancestors turn into men?
Swinging about in the family tree,
When did they start to look something like me?
Heavyweight brain, when did you grow?
Does anyone anywhere really know?

Who? Who can say who?
Who can unravel a riddle or two?
Melting the ice, unwinding the clocks,
Who'll take the lid off the mystery box?
Where do we come from and where do we go?
And who can say who is in charge of the show?
Does anyone anywhere really know?

*Julia Donaldson*


# Questions

. . . why does ice always feel cold
And why does anyone have to get old
And why are deserts always bone dry
And how do clouds stay up in the sky
And how do you know the earth is round
And how do worms breathe underground

And what do fishes drink
And why are snails so slow
And what do babies think
And where do shadows go

And how many drops in the ocean
And why's the horizon so far
And if atoms make up a person
Can people make up a star
And . . .

*Kevin McCann*

# SAYING SORRY

## *Sorry*

Why is the word 'sorry'
So very hard to say?
Your mouth goes dry,
Your arms go stiff,
Your knees start to give way.
And even when that little word
Is ready to pop out,
It rolls around
Upon your tongue
Until you have to shout,
'I'M SORRY!', just to get it past

Your gums, your teeth, your lips;
And then your mum says,
'Well, my girl,
It doesn't sound like it!'

*Coral Rumble*


## You Never Say Sorry First

It's true, you don't,
Even when it's your fault
(which it is most of the time),
It's always me that says sorry first,
Even when I've done nothing wrong,
I always say sorry first to try and smooth things over
Cos I don't like rows and sulky silence.
You could sulk for England you could,
That bottom lip's like a balcony,
And I can't stand the way you puff and pant dramatically
And throw your hair back while shaking your head
And stamping your foot.
You never admit anything,
You never say sorry first.

No it doesn't count now.
Don't say sorry just cos I asked you to,
Say sorry cos you want to.

I just wish you'd say sorry first,
Just once.

Apart from that, you're OK really.
Not bad for a best mate,
Even if you are a stubborn so-and-so.

*Paul Cookson*

# SEEING DIFFERENCE

## *Skin*

What is it about skin
that gets people so excited?

Skin is the body bag
that holds us together.

Skin is the smothering
that keeps out the weather.

Skin is the curtain
drawn down at the start.

Skin is the wrapper
that contains the heart.

Skin is the spray
round the ragbag of bone.

Skin is the sleeping bag
into which we are sewn.

Skin is thin –
even a rose thorn can rip skin

and yet some people
are afraid of it –

even though we are all made of it.

*Pie Corbett*

# SELF-BELIEF

## *The You Can Be ABC*

You can be
an artistic actor or a brainy barrister
a clever conductor or a dynamic dancer
an evil enemy or a fantastic friend
a green-fingered gardener or a healing herbalist
an interesting inventor or a jovial jolly juggler
a keen kitchen designer or a loggerheaded lumberjack
a melodious musician or a neat newsreader

an over-the-top opera singer or a princely-paid pop star
a quipping quiz master or a rich rugby player
a serious scientist or a typewriting traveller
an uppity umpire or a vigorous vet
a wonderful winner or an expert xylophonist
a yelling yachtsperson or a zealous zoologist.
So go to it, you can do it.
Someone's got to, why not you?
And who is going to stop you?
The only person who *can* stop you –
that's YOU!

*Roger Stevens*


# SHAME

## *Not the Answer*

Why is it
that when there's a fight
in the playground,
everyone gathers round
and starts taking sides,
even though most of them
don't know who started it
or what it's about?

Why is it
that when there's a fight
in the playground,
I join the others
and race to watch and cheer,
even though I know
deep down inside
fighting's not the answer?

*John Foster*

# STEALING

## *The Purse*

I pinched it from my mother's purse,
Pretending it's a game.
My muscles tightened: hard and tense.
I pinched it just the same.

'I need it as a loan,' I said.
'It's not against the law.'
'I won't do it again,' I said.
I've said all that before.

The reason was the cash at first,
It isn't any more;
I do it . . . well . . . because I do,
I don't know what it's for.

I only know that when the house
Is silent, empty, still,
I head towards my parents' room
As if against my will.

The sweat is cold upon my neck,
My back and arms feel strange,
I'm sure that someone's watching me
As I pick out her change.

But no one ever catches me,
Sometimes I wish they would;
Then perhaps I'd stop and think
And give it up for good.

But my mum trusts me, buys me things:
Each kindness makes it worse
Because I know, when she's next door
My hands will find her purse.

                              *David Kitchen*

# SULKING

## *Sulky in St Ives*

I must have been seven
when we went
to St Ives
for a holiday
and I nearly
drowned in the sea

Early afternoon
the tide was out
and I walked
on and on
till I finally got to
the sea

I kept going
till the water
came up
to my middle when suddenly
whoosh
the bottom of the sea
disappeared
and I went
down in the water
down with the bubbles

And I kept coming up
kept seeing them all
back on the beach
waving at me

And I kept going down
until one of them
came for me

And I cried
all the way back
to the beach
where everyone laughed
and laughed
at me

And I sulked
for the rest of the day
and I still get sulky
when I think
about it now

*James Carter*

# SPREADING JOY

## *If I Knew*

If I knew the box where the smiles are kept,
No matter how large the key
Or strong the bolt, I would try so hard
'Twould open I know for me,
Then over the land and sea broadcast
I'd scatter the smiles to play,
That the children's faces might hold them fast
For many and many a day.

If I knew the box that was large enough
To hold all the frowns I meet,
I would like to gather them every one
From the nursery, school or street,
Then, folding and holding, I'd pack them in
And turning the monster key,
I'd hire a giant to drop the box
To the depths of the deep, deep sea.

*Anon.*

# SURPRISES

## *Full of Surprises*

This poem is full of surprises
Each line holds something new
This poem is full of surprises
Especially for you . . .

It's full of tigers roaring
It's full of loud guitars
It's full of comets soaring
It's full of shooting stars

It's full of pirates fighting
It's full of winning goals
It's full of alien sightings
It's full of rock and roll

It's full of rainbows beaming
It's full of eagles flying
It's full of dreamers dreaming
It's full of teardrops drying

It's full of magic spells
It's full of wizards' pointy hats
It's full of fairy elves
It's full of witches and black cats

It's full of dragons breathing fire
It's full of dinosaurs
It's full of mountains reaching higher
It's full of warm applause

It's full of everything you need
It's full of more besides
It's full of food, the world to feed
It's full of fairground rides

It's full of love and happiness
It's full of dreams come true
It's full of things that are the best
Especially for you

It's jammed and crammed and packed and stacked
With things both old and new
This poem is full of surprises
Especially for you.

*Paul Cookson*

# TAKING TIME TO APPRECIATE THE WORLD

## *Leisure*

What is this life if, full of care,
We have no time to stand and stare?

No time to stand beneath the boughs
And stare as long as sheep or cows:

No time to see, when woods we pass,
Where squirrels hide their nuts in grass:

No time to see, in broad daylight,
Streams full of stars, like skies at night:

No time to turn at Beauty's glance,
And watch her feet, how they can dance:

No time to wait till her mouth can
Enrich that smile her eyes began?

A poor life this if, full of care,
We have no time to stand and stare.

*W. H. Davies*

# TEMPTATION

## *Temptation*

He'll never miss just one . . .
So I took it.
Then I lifted up the box and I shook it.
Seemed as heavy.
Sounded just as full.
All next day I felt that chocolate pull . . .

He'll never miss just one . . .
So I nicked it.
He'd never, never tell that I had picked it
Peeled the wrapper off and flicked it
Shiny in the bedroom bin.
All next day I knew the chocolate would win

A week on – and he's noticed.
Now he's twigged the box is light
And soon there'll be one big-time fight.
He'll guess who did it – and guess right.
For one and one and one and one
Kept adding on and on and on . . .
My last chance – like the chocolates – gone.

*Jan Dean*

# THINKING OF OTHERS

## *Inclusion*

In this class we
Never turn children away
Children learn and play
Laugh and love all together
Unique children
Sensitive to others' needs
In every school day
Only thinking of others
Nice if you join us

*Year 1, Whitfield & Aspen School, Dover*

# TRYING TO KEEP UP

## *In My Dream*

In my dream,
My older brother is racing along a sandy beach,
Whooping and laughing.

I am trying to keep up with him,
But he is drawing further and further away.

I call for him to wait,
But the wind whisks away my words.

When I tell my mother,
She hugs me.

'Don't worry,' she says.
'All in good time, your turn will come.'

*John Foster*

## VALUING WORDS

### Amazing Inventions

When I was 10
I really believed
that by the time
I was 20
there would be
such amazing inventions as
**FLYING CARS**
    **UNDERWATER CARS**
        **MACHINES**thatcouldmakeanyflavour
          *crisp*youaskedfor
day trips to the moon
video phones
            and robot dogs and cats
in e v e r y home
and
MOST IMPORTANTLY
## bubble gum
that could make you
# INVISIBLE

So you can also imagine
how extremely miffed Iwas
when I got to 40
and still none of them
had come true
either

Until they do
I'd like to say
do you know what
          I reckon
is the most **AMAZING INVENTION**
that us humans
have come up with so far?

Have a think

Our brains
come up with them

Our mouths
get rid of them

This poem is made of them

*James Carter*

# WANTING

## *The Want-Want Twins*

We are the Want-Want Twins.
We go from shop to shop.
We are the Want-Want Twins.
We don't know how to stop.
One day it's a bow and arrow.
Another it's a dinosaur.
What are we going to get tomorrow?
More. More. More.

We are the Want-Want Twins.
Our eyes sharp shiny pins.
Our hands quick shark's fins.
We go from shop to shop.
One day it's the game *Frustration*.
We don't know what we need.
Another it is compensation.
Greed. Greed. Greed.

We are the Want-Want Twins.
We're completely over the top.
We are the Want-Want Twins.
We don't know how to stop.
We send our parents every night
A list that goes like this:
2 new bikes. Don't be tight.
X.X.X.

We are the Want-Want Twins.
Money grows on trees.
We are the Want-Want Twins.
We are the bee's knees.
All we want is everything.
We don't know how to stop.
We will be the Want-Want Twins till we

drop

    drop

      drop.

*Jackie Kay*

# WISHING

## *Seven Wishes*

Why can't I be the band that ties your forehead,
so close to your thoughts?

Why can't I be the nub of sweetcorn
you shred with your wildcat's teeth?

Why can't I be the turquoise round your neck
warmed by the storm of your blood?

Why can't I be the thread of many colours
that slides through your fingers on the loom?

Why can't I be the velvet tunic
over the ebb and flow of your heart?

Why can't I be the sand in your moccasins
that dares to stroke your toes?

Why can't I be your night's dream
when you moan in the black arms of sleep?

*Traditional, Pueblo Indians of New Mexico*

# I wish . . .

I wish I could be small enough
To wear a foxglove for a hat.

I wish I could sleep all night
Under a roof tile and chatter
To the sparrows that nest there.

I wish I could be a dragonfly
And hover like a miniature helicopter
Across the school pond.

I wish I could hide inside
a hermit crab's shell
and keep the world at bay.

I wish I could wear a snail's shell
To protect me from angry words.

I wish I could be a note
In an eagle's call as it hovers
High above the mountain's edge.

I wish I could blossom on a gorse bush
And smell of yellow coconut.

I wish I could be an apple seed
So that I could grow an orchard.

I wish I could be the pause
Just before an unkind word is spoken
So that I could stretch that silence.

I wish that I could be
The moment when a laugh takes root
And blossoms in your mouth
And I'd stay there forever
Trapped in that moment of sweet light.

*Pie Corbett*

# WONDER

## *Wilderness*

Miss says wilderness
is beautiful, natural, endless . . .
is space.

Mum's *Oxford English Dictionary* states:
'wild or uncultivated land'.

At the end of our garden
there's a lime tree.
I climb it, high as I can.

Sometimes
I sit up there for hours,
especially in the dark
staring at the stars,
touching wilderness,

out there
and inside me.

*Joan Poulson*

# WONDERING ABOUT THE FUTURE

## *A Map of Me*

What I want
is a map of me –
my future
and my destiny

My who I'll be
my where I'll go
my what I'll do
and need to know

My what I'll see
my what I'll say
my how I'll feel
along the way

But should I wait
for such a thing –
or go and see
what life will bring?

*James Carter*

# WORRYING ABOUT TESTS

## *A Pupil's Prayer*

Let me get in awful trouble,
let my school shoes grow too tight.
Let my bubbly not blow bubbles,
but,
let my sums be right.

May my birthday be forgotten,
may it rain all weekend long.
May I fall and bruise my bottom,
but please,
may my spellings not be wrong.

Let me lose my brand-new pencil case,
let my felt-tips all get nicked.
Let aunties kiss me all over my face,
but please, please,
let my tables all be ticked.

May there be no chocolate-chip ice cream,
may fleas invade my vest.
May I not get chosen for the team,
but please, please, please,
may I survive this rotten test.

*David Horner*

# God Be in My Head

God be in my head,
And in my understanding;

God be in my eyes,
And in my looking;

God be in my mouth,
And in my speaking;

God be in my head,
And in my thinking;

God be at my end,
And at my departing.

*Sarum Missal*

# People – Families and Friends, Heroes and Heroines

## When the Heart

When the heart is hard and parched up,
come upon me with a shower of mercy.
When grace is lost from life,
come with a burst of song.

*Rabindranath Tagore*

## People Need People

To walk to
To talk to
To cry and rely on,
People will always need people.
To love and to miss
To hug and to kiss,
It's useful to have other people.
To whom will you moan
If you're all alone,
It's so hard to share
When no one is there,
There's not much to do
When there's no one but you,
People will always need people.

To please
To tease
To put you at ease,
People will always need people.
To make life appealing
And give life some meaning,
It's useful to have other people.
If you need change
To whom will you turn,
If you need a lesson
From whom will you learn,
If you need to play
You'll know why I say
People will always need people.

As girlfriends
As boyfriends,
From Bombay
To Ostend,
People will always need people.
To have friendly fights with
And share tasty bites with,
It's useful to have other people.
People live in families
Gangs, posses and packs,
It seems we need company
Before we relax,
So stop making enemies
And let's face the facts,

People will always need people,
Yes
People will always need people.

*Benjamin Zephaniah*

## Smiles Like Roses

All down my street
smiles opened like roses
Sun licked me and tickled me
Sun said, *Didn't you believe me*
*when I said I'd be back?*

I blinked my eyes, I said,
*Sun, you are too strong for me*
*where'd you get those muscles?*
Sun said, *Come and dance.*

All over the park
smiles opened like roses
babies kicked off their shoes
and sun kissed their toes.

All those new babies
all that new sun
everybody dancing
walking but dancing.

185

All over the world
Sun kicked off his shoes
and came home dancing
licking and tickling,

kissing crossing-ladies and fat babies
saying to everyone,
*Hey you are the most beautiful*
*dancing people I've ever seen*
*with those smiles like roses!*

Helen Dunmore

## Our Sounds

The people in our family
each have a favourite sound.
Dad chinks the money in his pocket,
5p, 10p, pound.
I like the bell of my new blue bike
and the rattle of the doorkeys.
The dog likes to hear the car come home
and a voice that calls out 'Walkies'.
Kate likes to hear the rain drum
and the buzzing of the phone,
and Mum . . . ? She loves the silence
when she's in all on her own.

*Sue Cowling*

# Just Mum and Me

We didn't do anything special today,
just Mum and me.
Raining outside, nowhere to go,
just Mum and me.

So we baked and talked and talked and baked
and baked and talked,
just Mum and me.

She told me about when she was young
and how her gran baked exactly the same cakes
on rainy days and baked and talked to her.

She remembered her friends
and the games they used to play,
the trees they used to climb,
the blackberries they picked,
the fields they used to run around in
and how summers always seemed to be sunny.

And Mum smiled a smile I don't often see,
the years falling away from her face,
and just for a moment
I caught a glimpse of the girl she used to be.

We didn't do anything special today,
raining outside, nowhere to go,
so we baked and talked and talked and baked,
just Mum and me.

I ate and listened and listened and ate,
the hours racing by so quickly.

We didn't do anything special . . .
but it was special, really special.

Just Mum and me.

*Paul Cookson*


## Fostered

She was a mother to me,
the loveliest there ever could be
was Joey.

I wasn't her own,
she had none, I was sort of on loan
to Joey.

But the time that we shared
was great, for she cared,
did Joey.

And all through my childhood
I learnt what a child should
from Joey.

I learnt respect for all creatures
from this kindest of teachers,
dear Joey.

Now I am called Mum
and I've tried hard to become
like Joey, my Joey.

*Catherine Benson*


# Walking Home with My Foster Father

My hand in his and both inside his pocket.
Six years old and out at night, walking home.
Frost haloes ringed each street-lamp,
Round rainbows of yellow-green.
Cold air rasped my lungs.
Pavements glittered ice.

Our boots left hot black prints in white rime.
My toes would not separate.
The moon puffed cloud vapour across stars.
The world seemed bigger with its blue peeled back.
He'd told me once, 'Out there . . . that's Space.'
Rough tweed scratched my wrist.

His hand was very warm.
The smell of sawn logs seeped from his overalls.
'Look, there's the Plough,' he said.
'And there's the Giant.'
A giant farming the sky, I thought,
And stared at the fields of space.

*Catherine Benson*


# Stepmother

My Stepmother
      is really nice.
She ought to wear
      a label.
I don't come in
      with a latch key now –
my tea is on
      the table.
She doesn't nag at me
      or shout.
I often hear her
      singing.
I'm glad my dad
      had wedding bells –
and I hope
      they go on ringing.

Stepmothers
        in fairy tales
are hard and cold
        as iron.
There isn't a lie
        they wouldn't tell,
or a trick
        they wouldn't try on.
But MY stepmother's
        warm and true;
she's kind, and cool,
        and clever –
Yes! I've a *wicked*
        stepmother –
and I hope she stays
        forever!

*Jean Kenward*

## Father's Hands

Father's hands
large like frying pans
broad as shovel blades
strong as weathered spades.

Father's hands
finger ends ingrained with dirt
permanently stained from work
ignoring pain and scorning hurt.

I once saw him walk boldly up to a swan
that had landed in next door's drive and wouldn't move.
The police were there because swans are a protected
   species
but didn't do anything, but my dad walked up to it,
picked it up and carried it away. No problem.
Those massive wings that can break a man's bones
were held tight, tight by my father's hands
and I was proud of him that day, really proud.

Father's hands
tough as leather on old boots
firmly grasping nettle shoots
pulling thistles by their roots.

Father's hands
gripping like an iron vice
never numb in snow and ice
nails and screws are pulled and prised.

He once found a kestrel with a broken wing
and kept it in our garage until it was better.
He'd feed it by hand with scraps of meat or dead mice
and you could see where its beak and talons
had taken bits of skin from his finger ends.

It never seemed to hurt him at all, he just smiled
as he let it claw and peck.

Father's hands
lifting bales of hay and straw
calloused, hardened, rough and raw
building, planting, painting . . . more.

Father's hands
hard when tanning my backside
all we needed they supplied
and still my hands will fit inside

Father's hands
large like frying pans
broad as shovel blades
strong as weathered spades.

And still my hands will fit inside
my father's hands.

*Paul Cookson*

# My Dad

My dad's not a teacher
a ghost or a ghoul,
he isn't a spaceman,
a jester or fool.

He doesn't walk tightropes
or dance on hot coals,
play for United
or score lots of goals.

He isn't a rock star
a wizard or king,
he isn't a builder
and he can't really sing.

He doesn't do time walks
or cook on TV,
write silly poems
or make cups of tea.

My dad isn't wealthy
he's not strong or wild,
but my dad is special
and I am his child.

*Peter Dixon*

## *My Dad Is Amazing!*

My dad's **amazing** for he can:

make mountains out of molehills,
teach Granny to suck eggs,
make Mum's blood boil
and then drive her up the wall.

My dad's **amazing** for he also:

walks around with his head in the clouds,
has my sister eating out of his hand,
says he's got eyes in the back of his head
and can read me like a book.

But,
the most **amazing** thing of all is:

when he's caught someone red-handed,
first he jumps down their throat
and then he bites their head off!

*Ian Souter*

# *Together*

On holiday it's different – there's a different side to Dad.
No phone, no letters, no work,
he just unwinds, lets it all hang out,
has the time to finish conversations,
the time to finish the newspaper and not just the sports
  page,
the time to laugh and joke,
the time to play our silly games,
the time to travel backwards and become a child with us.

The time to muck about,
splash water, kick footballs,
eat fish and chips, ice cream and pizza in the same
  afternoon,
the time to get told off by Mum
for being silly and setting us a bad example
(although she doesn't really mean it).

But best of all . . .
the time to be together.

*Paul Cookson*

## Mum and Dad Are Mum and Dad

Mum and dad are mum and dad.
Well, they are . . . but in some way they're not.
You see, although they didn't actually
bring me into this world
they did bring me up in this world.

Adopted at birth
mum and dad are mum and dad
and always have been.

Never once have I wanted to go back,
trace the roots and dig up the past.
Never once have I wanted to question
face to face and flesh to flesh
with whoever brought me into this world
and then let me go.

What has been is.
What will be is.
What is is.
And never once have I wanted to change it.

Mum and dad are mum and dad.
Always have been
and always will be.

They chose me
and if I had a choice
I know with all my heart
that I could not have chosen better.

*Paul Cookson*

## A Parent's Prayer

Always believe in yourself.
Promise always to be compassionate.
Appreciate that you make mistakes,
Recognize that I do too.
Entrust me with your worries.
Never doubt that I will support you when you need me.
Talk to me about the things you find difficult.
Share your dreams.

Please understand that I can have moods just like you.
Receive a little advice now and again.
Accept that I sometimes get things wrong.
You need to help me to get things right.
Enjoy your life.
Realize that I love you without reservation.

*Gervase Phinn*

## Brother's Best at Sandcastles

Brother's best at sandcastles,
Loves the details and the plans,
Sticks and stones and shells are magic in his hands.

Like a sculptor sculpting,
A work of art displayed,
No hammer and no chisel, just a bucket and a spade.

Mine just crumble, mine just fall,
Ruins with no style at all.
His are full of moats and towers,
He works on them for hours and hours.

They may be something special
But even they cannot withstand
The ever creeping tide smoothing out the sand.

*Paul Cookson*

## Sarah, My Sister, Has Asthma

Sarah, my sister, has asthma.
Sometimes, I wake up in the night
And hear her wheezing
In the bunk below.

I remember the time
I woke to hear her gasping for breath
And Mum had to call an ambulance.
They took her to the hospital
And kept her in for tests.

'She's allergic,' the doctor said.
'I expect she'll grow out of it.
Most young children do.'

Now she carries an inhaler
Everywhere she goes.

She gets annoyed when people
Try to stop her doing things.
She's always telling Grandma
To stop fussing.

'I'm not different,' she says.
'It's only asthma.
Lots of people have it.'

On Sports Day
Sarah came first in the high jump.
'You see, I'm not different,' she said.

Sarah, my sister, has asthma.
Sometimes I wake up in the night
And hear her wheezing
In the bunk below.

*John Foster*

## Fishing with Uncle John

The two of us, five o'clock in the morning
and the sunrise pulling back
the misty water's blanket.

Not a sound, save the whirr of reels,
the swish of lines and the plop of bait,
not that we caught anything.

Eventually, the bird song
and hum of bugs invisible,
the occasional mini chainsaw buzz of bees
or the gloating splash of free fish.

The roll of Uncle's eyes at our failure,
the crazy smile of 'Why are we here?!'
and the fish and chips in the car on the way home.

*Paul Cookson*

## Marjorie

She was short-sighted and wore glasses.
She was a Sunday School teacher.
She was engaged to a soldier.
She had her picture taken in a grey dress.

She died at twenty-one of scarlet fever.
She was buried on Christmas Eve.
This is all I know about her,
The aunt I never knew, my mother's sister.
Is it my face or hers in the mirror?
Her face or mine in the frame?
And whom do they see when they look at me?

*Sue Cowling*

## My Sparrow Gran

My sparrow gran
Is the singing one
Busy and tidy
And brown-bright-eyed
She chirrups and chats
She scurries and darts
She picks up the bits
That clutter her nest
And when evening comes
When all her work's done
I bring her my book
And sit on her lap
Snug in her arms
That are feather-down warm.

*Berlie Doherty*

# No One Made Mash Like My Grandad!

With a fork and some
pepper, butter and cream –

in front of the fire
he whipped up a dream.

*Rupert M. Loydell*

# If All The World Were Paper

If all the world were paper,
I would fold up my granny
and take her everywhere I go.
I would laminate my baby sister in bubble wrap,
lay her to sleep in unbound fairy tale book pages,
and should she get scared . . .
Rip every yell
Tear every scream
Shred every fear.

If all the world were paper
I would rebind my grandfather,
Smooth out the creases to all his stories
place his younger days in a zoetrope
and flush the harrowing chapters
down an ink gurgling well.

If all the world were paper
birthday cards and christmas wrapping foil
would follow you to school.
Arguments would rustle before they started
and could be put right
with a little tape.

If all the world were paper
dreams would be braille
so we could read them whilst we slept,
nightmares would be shopping lists,
shopping lists are easy to forget.

If all the world were paper
we could paperclip families together
draw smiles on all the sad faces
rub out the tears
cover our homes in Tipp-Ex
and start all over again.

All the world is not paper
but whilst we can imagine it were,
we can recycle the rough times
and never, ever fold.

*Joseph Coelho*

## Mercy

Mercy her name was,
The blind lady.
Took her home from bingo
Each Wednesday night,
With her stick tap-rapping
On the breeze-blocks.
She'd humour and love.
No sight.

And suddenly
I recall
Salt of a tide of darkness
Swirling up under that door
She swam through with her key
And turned no light on.
Why should she?
She left all light
Behind her,
Needing none
To find things there:
Things, it seemed,
Could find her.

Mercy.
Took her home from bingo
Each Wednesday night,
With her stick tap-rapping

On the breeze-blocks.
Mercy.
Heart of light.

*Kit Wright*

## *You Find Out Who Your Friends Are*

We all admired her.
She was in the year above us.
Glamorous.
So when she picked me out to mock
And said *that thing*
In front of all the others
Everyone fell silent.
Numb, too shocked to cry
I felt as if she'd slapped me.
Nightmare of an afternoon.
No one said, 'You OK?'
But when I walked out through the gate
You were the one
Who walked with me.
My mate.

*Sue Cowling*

# For Now

If I can change the world for you
one day,
won't that be grand!

For now I'll fetch the tissues,
mop your tears
and hold your hand.

*Sue Cowling*

# Best Friends (Not)

When my best friend and I fall out
We stand miles apart
Talking loudly
To people we don't think are special

When my best friend and I make up
We stand very close
Talking quietly
About the things we think are special.

*John Coldwell*

## *With You, Without You*

With you I'm one of the fearless two
Without you I'm the cautious one.

With you I think I'm the queen of the dancefloor
Without you I'm just a clumsy ugly sister.

With you my name is complete
Without you it's just waiting for the *and*.

With you I feel a hundred per cent
Without you I'm less than fifty.

With you I can take on the world
Without you I just wish you are here.

With you I know that you feel the same
Without you I know that you feel the same.

With you, without you
We are the perfect team.

*Paul Cookson*

## You Are

The Oxo in the gravy,
the Bisto in my stew,
the custard on my pudding,
the window with a view.

You're the prezzie in the cracker,
you're the apple in the pie,
the answer to the question,
the twinkle in the eye.

You're the magic in the secret,
my firework in the night,
my sunshine in the morning,
the sum that's always right.

You are neither rich nor famous
but to me you are the best –
you're the head upon my pillow
and the paw upon my chest.

*Peter Dixon*

## Letter to a Friend
### (Not to be opened for 50 years)

Do you remember the pit?
Our hang-out, where we swung
on old matted rope,
out over logs that held our imagination
and shaped our thoughts.
Those logs were wizards and witches;
and the tangled mass of roots
looked like old tennis racquet strings.
But they were sturdy and covered in clay,
moulded over an old man's face.
Do you remember freestyle biking
on my tricycle,
or walking on in the stream?
Each step cracked the ice, leaving footprints
spiked by frost.
Do you remember
sliding down our hill on plastic bags in the snow?
We were dressed for the Arctic
but soon we were hot and slid down the hill
in T-shirts and trousers.
When you read this
you will probably have forgotten me . . .
I will be an old school friend
and nothing more.
But when you read this

your crocheted web of memories
may hold Emma and Hannah,
the inseparable pair.

*Hannah Edwards, aged 13*

## Gracefully

Every day
my friend
spends many hours in a wheelchair
– got to rock and roll,
be on the go

I love the way he burns rubber when he's in a hurry
and just
enjoy the whole movement
when he turns
those wheels real slow.

Doctors said
his legs weren't strong enough to carry him
and for a long time
he felt this wasn't fair
when people next door,
people at school,
people on the television
all walked sort of upright in the air.

He said to me,
'I know, you
want to ask me how I feel
and how it is
that I don't often wear a frown
but it makes me laugh to know
that people with all this leg power
spend most of their time
looking to sit down!'

We've played snooker
together.
He uses extra cushions
for a little more height at the table
but there are no ramps
for easier access,
in fact it's like that most places we go to.

He says,
'Temporary able-bodied people
don't like the idea of wheelchairs.
It makes them feel uncomfortable
I suppose they'd prefer me to stay at home
and cause
their lives less trouble.'

He says,
'But this world
belongs as much to me,
what I cannot walk on
I can roll on just as gracefully.'

Every day
my friend
spends many hours in a wheelchair,
wheeling to a stop and spin.
I love the way he burns rubber
but most of all
I love him for being him, so very . . .
gracefully.

*Abraham Gibson*

## Never

I never saw his smile
I always saw the glasses and hearing aid

I never saw her sparkling eyes
I always saw the wheelchair

I never heard his words of kindness
I always heard the cleft lip

I never heard her laugh
I always heard the stammer

I never saw and never heard
I never got too close.

*Paul Cookson*

# Harry

I remember it like it was yesterday, Harry.
The aching cold of the northern air
dusting the Keiss cloakroom floor,
my house miles away, somewhere,
beyond the funeral face of the school building,
and you standing at the door –
twelve years old, staring and eight feet tall.
Then you slowly walked in.

I remember the other boys,
frozen, fixed against the wall
in the headlamp of your stare
and me, soaked to the skin and
trying to look elsewhere.
They thought it would be funny,
to choose someone in his first day at school
for the basin trick.

'Look in here, mate! There's a special surprise . . .'
I had stretched up, until my believing eyes
saw over the thick, cold sink edge.
I had stared for a second,
before the older hands scooped the water
into my face and down through my clothes.
I know you saw them laughing, and
then they saw you and ran.

That's when it happened.
That's when it happened.
I remember the rough feel of your jumper
drying my legs, my hair, my face.
I remember the tough feel of your hand
taking me back to my place.
The sound of your footsteps on
the polished classroom boards
and the feeling of safety,
wrapped warmly in your words:
'You're fine . . .' you whispered,
'You're fine.'

When you are old and grey and
your grandchildren ask you about
your life and what you have done . . .
Yes, tell them about the jobs and the hobbies,
tell them about the travelling and the towns,
the mistakes and the triumphs . . .
But tell them about that day, Harry.
Tell them about our day;
about the four-year-old boy in that cloakroom . . .
who still sees you standing in the doorway,
still sees you take off that old jumper,
still sees you stretch out your hand.

*Mark Halliday*

## Bullies and Their Messengers

Have you noticed how bullies always have gangs
and never ever walk alone?
They never speak to you one to one,
it's always some little messenger
who comes up to you and says,
'Watchityordedcosmybigmate'sgonnagetyouRIGHT!'

Bullies' messengers are always small.
Always.
By themselves they're nothing, nobodies,
who hide in shadows on the way home,
never saying boo to a goose
. . . but when they're with their big mates
they think they are big hard tough guy fighters
who say big hard tough guy things like,
    'IfyoutouchmeI'llgetmybigmateontoyouSOWATCHIT!'

Bullies and their messengers
are always always small people inside,
hiding in large groups,
pretending that they're really tough
when really they are frightened nobodies
scared to be alone,
and if by chance you do catch them alone
they will be just as scared as you might be
and they will be just as likely to walk away silently
as they are to start a fight with you

because bullies and their messengers are cowards
yes, bullies and their messengers are cowards
and that, my friends, is very very true.

*Paul Cookson*


## Dobbo's First Swimming Lesson

Dobbo's fists
spiked me to the playground wall
nailed me to the railings.

The plastic ball
he kicked against my skinny legs
on winter playtimes

Bounced a stinging red-hot bruise
across the icy tarmac.

The day we started swimming
we all jumped in
laughed and splashed, sank beneath
the funny-tasting water.

Shivering in a corner
Dobbo crouched, stuck to the side,
sobbing like my baby brother
when all the lights go out.

*David Harmer*

217

## *Matilda*
### *who told lies, and was burned to death*

Matilda told such Dreadful Lies,
It made one Gasp and Stretch one's Eyes;
Her Aunt, who, from her Earliest Youth,
Had kept a Strict Regard for Truth,
Attempted to Believe Matilda:
The effort very nearly killed her,
And would have done so, had not She
Discovered this Infirmity.
For once, towards the Close of Day,
Matilda, growing tired of play,
And finding she was left alone,
Went tiptoe to the Telephone
And summoned the Immediate Aid
Of London's Noble Fire-Brigade.
Within an hour the Gallant Band
Were pouring in on every hand,
From Putney, Hackney Downs and Bow,
With Courage high and Hearts a-glow
They galloped, roaring through the Town,
'Matilda's House is Burning Down!'
Inspired by British Cheers and Loud
Proceeding from the Frenzied Crowd,
They ran their ladders through a score
Of windows on the Ballroom Floor;
And took Peculiar Pains to Souse
The Pictures up and down the house,

Until Matilda's Aunt succeeded
In showing them they were not needed
And even then she had to pay
To get the Men to go away!

It happened that a few Weeks later
Her Aunt was off to the Theatre
To see that interesting Play
*The Second Mrs Tanqueray.*
She had refused to take her Niece
To hear this Entertaining Piece:
A Deprivation Just and Wise
To Punish her for Telling Lies.
That Night a Fire *did* break out –
You should have heard Matilda Shout!
You should have heard her Scream and Bawl,
And throw the window up and call
To People passing in the Street –
(The rapidly increasing Heat
Encouraging her to obtain
Their confidence) – but all in vain!
For every time She shouted 'Fire!'
They only answered 'Little Liar!'
And therefore when her Aunt returned,
Matilda, and the House, were Burned.

*Hilaire Belloc*

# Mister Moore

Mister Moore, Mister Moore
Creaking down the corridor.

Uh uh eh eh uh
Uh uh eh eh uh

Mister Moore wears wooden suits
Mister Moore's got great big boots
Mister Moore's got hair like a brush
And Mister Moore don't like me much.

Mister Moore, Mister Moore
Creaking down the corridor.

Uh uh eh eh uh
Uh uh eh eh uh

When my teacher's there I haven't got a care
I can do my sums, I can do gerzinters
When Mister Moore comes through the door
Got a wooden head filled with splinters.

Mister Moore, Mister Moore
Creaking down the corridor.

Uh uh eh eh uh
Uh uh eh eh uh

Mister Moore I implore
My earholes ache, my head is sore
Don't come through that classroom door.
Don't come through that classroom door.

Mister Moore, Mister Moore
Creaking down the corridor.

Uh uh eh eh uh
Uh uh eh eh uh

Big voice big hands
Big feet he's a very big man
Take my advice, be good be very very nice
Be good be very very nice
Mister Moore, Mister Moore
Creaking down the corridor.

Uh uh eh eh uh
Uh uh eh eh uh

Mister Moore wears wooden suits
Mister Moore's got great big boots
Mister Moore's got hair like a brush
And Mister Moore don't like me much.

Mister Moore, Mister Moore
Creaking down the corridor.

Uh uh eh eh uh
Uh uh eh eh uh

*David Harmer*

## A Visit to Casualty

In casualty there's a nurse with 'Jesus fingers' –
She touches gently and strokes away pain.
She has long, calming fingers –
As delicate as spider silk,
Smoothed at the ends by acts of kindness.
Each finger is clean, but some are marked,
Scarred by years of caring.

Her fingers are strong, you can depend on them.
They hold tightly to your hand as you walk down to
   X-ray,
They firmly cradle your head when the doctor prods.
If you cry, you can be sure one of those fingers
Will dry your tears.

They are fingers that steady you if you lose your balance,
They play games with you to make you smile.
They softly lift strands of hair away from your eyes
And carefully wash dirt from the sore bits.

Grown-ups probably won't notice her Jesus fingers
Cos they find it hard to see through the eyes of their spirit,
They don't like to be touched by the unusual.

*Coral Rumble*

## Mir Baku

Mir Baku lives at number 22.
He wears a curled-wool, ship-shaped hat
pulled down over his large, furled ears.
He never takes it off
as far as I can see.
He walks to the corner shop
every morning
hunched into his overcoat
(the one with a rip and loads of pockets).
Then he walks back
with a funny-written newspaper, two small tins of catfood,
a loaf of lumpy black bread and four onions.
Dad says he came from the Soviet Union.
But where's that, nowadays?
Is he a Kazakh? An Uzbek? A Chechen?
Or is he from Azerbaijan?
I'd like to ask,
but Mum says it'd be rude.
So I just call 'Good Morning,'
and watch the fierce brown crinkles
round his eyes
as he smiles at the cats in his window.

*Lucy Coats*

# Optimistic Man

as a child he never plucked the wings off flies
he didn't tie tin cans to cats' tails
or lock beetles in matchboxes
or stomp anthills
he grew up
and all those things were done to him
I was at his bedside when he died
he said read me a poem
about the sun and the sea
about nuclear reactors and satellites
about the greatness of humanity

*Nazim Hikmet*
*(translated by Randy Blasing*
*and Mutlu Konuk)*

# Harriet Tubman
*Freedom Fighter*
*About 1823–1913*
*Maryland, USA*

'Miss Moses' people called her,
For she was very brave.
She opened the doors of freedom
To help the hopeful slave.

She led her folk from bondage
On many, many trips;
A gun beneath her cloak but
A prayer on her lips!

Sometimes they grew so frightened
Their bodies quaked with fears.
She nudged them with her gun and
Then wiped away their tears!

She slipped behind the Rebel lines;
A Union spy was she,
She burned their crops and freed their slaves,
Then left to set more free!

*Eloise Crosby Culver*

## Have Mercy on Me

Have mercy on me, O Beneficent One, I was angered for I
had no shoes:
Then I met a man who had no feet.

*Chinese saying*
*(Translated Anon.)*

## *People*

Some of us eat
Birds meats or
Escargots or
Candied bees or
Each other –
   But we are all people

Some of us carry
Bibles or
Rifles or
Swastikas or
Spears or
Bows and arrows or
Love signs –
   But we are all people

Some of us wear
Sarongs or
Feathers or
Cheong sams or
Muu muus or
Dior creations or
Nothing –
   But we are all people

Some of us dance
Waltzes or
Ballets or
Corroborees or
Hulas or
Bossa nova or
Flamenco –
   We are all people.

*Bobbi Sykes*


## We Shall Overcome

We shall overcome.
We shall overcome.
We shall overcome some day.
Oh Darling,
Deep in my heart, I do believe,
We shall overcome some day.

We'll walk hand in hand.
We'll walk hand in hand.
We'll walk hand in hand some day.
Oh Darling,
Deep in my heart, I do believe,
We'll walk hand in hand some day.

We shall live in peace.
We shall live in peace.
We shall live in peace some day.
Oh Darling,
Deep in my heart, I do believe,
We shall live in peace some day.

We are not afraid.
We are not afraid.
We shall overcome some day.
Oh Darling,
Deep in my heart, I do believe,
We shall overcome some day.

*Protest song*

# The Most Important Rap

I am an astronaut
I circle the stars
I walk on the moon
I travel to Mars
I'm brave and tall
There is nothing I fear
and I am the most important person here.

I am a teacher
I taught you it all
I taught you why your
spaceship doesn't fall
If you couldn't read or write
where would you be?
The most important person here is me.

Who are you kidding?
Are you taking the mick?
Who makes you better
when you're feeling sick?
I am a doctor
and I'm always on call
and I am more important than you all.

But I'm your mother
Don't forget me
If it wasn't for your mother
where would you be?
I washed your nappies
and changed your vest
I'm the most important
and mummy knows best.

I am a child
and the future I see
and there'd be no future
if it wasn't for me

I hold the safety
of the planet in my hand
I'm the most important
and you'd better understand.

Now just hold on
I've a message for you all
Together we stand
and divided we fall
So let's make a circle
and all remember this
Who's the most important?
Everybody is.
Who's the most important?
EVERYBODY IS!

*Roger Stevens*

# from *The Sermon on the Mount*

Blessed are the poor in spirit:
For theirs is the kingdom of heaven.

Blessed are they that mourn:
For they shall be comforted.

Blessed are the meek:
For they shall inherit the earth.

Blessed are they which do hunger and thirst after
  righteousness:
For they shall be filled.

Blessed are the merciful:
For they shall obtain mercy.

Blessed are the pure in heart:
For they shall see God.

Blessed are the peacemakers:
For they shall be called the children of God.

Blessed are they which are persecuted for righteousness'
  sake:
For theirs is the kingdom of heaven.

*King James Bible*

# A Jewish Prayer

May the Lord bless you and keep you.
May the Lord's face shine upon you.
May the Lord be gracious unto you.
May the Lord give you peace,
From this day forth
And for evermore.

*Traditional Jewish*

## from *The Method of Prayer*

Those who read fast reap no more advantage than a bee would by only skimming over the surface of the flower.

*Madame Guyon*

# Looking After
# the World

## Yoruba Poem

Enjoy the earth gently
Enjoy the earth gently
For if the earth is spoiled
It cannot be repaired
Enjoy the earth gently

*Anon.*

## The Summer Day

Who made the world?
Who made the swan, and the black bear?
Who made the grasshopper?
This grasshopper, I mean –
the one who has flung herself out of the grass,
the one who is eating sugar out of my hand,
who is moving her jaws back and forth instead of up and
    down –
who is gazing around with her enormous and complicated
    eyes.
Now she lifts her pale forearms and thoroughly washes her
    face.
Now she snaps her wings open, and floats away.
I don't know exactly what a prayer is.
I do know how to pay attention, how to fall down
into the grass, how to kneel down in the grass,
how to be idle and blessed, how to stroll through the
    fields,

which is what I have been doing all day.
Tell me, what else should I have done?
Doesn't everything die at last, and too soon?
Tell me, what is it you plan to do
with your one wild and precious life?

*Mary Oliver*


# How Can You Buy the Sky?

How can you buy the sky?
How can you own the rain and wind?

My mother told me,
Every part of this earth is sacred to our people.
Every pine needle. Every sandy shore.
Every mist in the dark woods.
Every meadow and humming insect.
All are holy in the memory of our people.

My father told me,
I know the sap that courses through the trees
as I know the blood that flows in my veins.
We are part of the earth and it is part of us.
The perfumed flowers are our sisters.
The bear, the deer, the great eagle, these are our brothers.
The rocky crests, the meadows, the ponies – all belong to
   the same family.

The voice of my ancestors said to me,
The shining water that moves in the streams and rivers
is not simply water, but the blood of your grandfather's
  grandfather.
Each ghostly reflection in the clear waters of the lake
tells of memories in the life of our people.
The water's murmur is the voice of your great-great-
  grandmother.
The rivers are our brothers. They quench our thirst.
They carry our canoes and feed our children.
You must give the rivers kindness
you would give to any brother.

The voice of my grandfather said to me,
The air is precious. It shares its spirit with all the life it
  supports.
The wind that gave me my first breath also received my
  last sigh.
You must keep the land and air apart and sacred,
as a place where one can go to taste the wind
that is sweetened by the meadow flowers.

When the last Red Man and Woman have vanished with
  their wilderness,
and their memory is only the shadow of a cloud moving
  across the prairie, will the shores and forest still be here?
Will there be any of the spirit of my people left?
My ancestors said to me, This we know:
The earth does not belong to us. We belong to the earth.

*Chief Seattle*

## *The Earth and the People*

The earth was here before the people.
The very first people
came out of the ground.
Everything came from the ground,
even caribou.
Children once grew
out of the ground
just as flowers do.
Women out wandering
found them sprawling on the grass
and took them home and nursed them.
That way people multiplied.

This land of ours
has become habitable
because we came here
and learned how to hunt.

*Traditional Inuit*

# Iroquois Prayer

We return thanks to our mother, the earth,
   which sustains us.
We return thanks to the rivers and streams,
   which supply us with water.
We return thanks to all herbs, which furnish
   medicines for the cure of our diseases.
We return thanks to the corn, and to her sisters,
   the beans and squashes, which give us life.
We return thanks to the bushes and trees,
   which provide us with fruit.
We return thanks to the wind, which,
   moving the air, has banished diseases.
We return thanks to the moon and stars,
   which have given to us their light
   when the sun was gone.
We return thanks to our grandfather Hé-no,
   that he has protected his grandchildren from
   witches and reptiles, and has given to us his rain.
We return thanks to the sun, that he has looked upon
   the earth with a beneficent eye.
Lastly, we return thanks to the Great Spirit,
   in whom is embodied all goodness, and who
   directs all things for the good of his children.

*Anon.*

## Song of the Sky Loom

O our Mother the Earth, O our Father the Sky,
Your children are we, and with tired backs
We bring you the gifts you love.
Then weave for us a garment of brightness;
May the warp be the white light of morning,
May the weft be the red light of evening,
May the fringes be the falling rain,
May the border be the standing rainbow.
Thus weave for us a garment of brightness,
That we may walk fittingly where grass is green,
O our Mother the Earth, O our Father the Sky.

*Traditional Tewa (North American Indian)*

## My Moccasins Have Not Walked

My moccasins have not walked
Among the giant forest trees

My leggings have not brushed
Against the fern and berry bush

My medicine pouch has not been filled
with roots and herbs and sweetgrass

My hands have not fondled the spotted fawn

My eyes have not beheld
The golden rainbow of the north

My hair has not been adorned
With the eagle feather

Yet
My dreams are dreams of these
My heart is one with them
The scent of them caresses my soul

*Duke Redbird*


## Prayer

Let me walk in the fields and the forest
In a land that is rich and fair
Let me swim in the cool, clean ocean
Let me breathe untainted air

Let the sun's rays warm my body
Let the sun's light into my soul
Let us pray for this damaged planet
That one day it will heal and be whole

*Roger Stevens*

# Give and Take

I give you clean air
You give me poisonous gas.
I give you mountains
You give me quarries.

I give you pure snow
You give me acid rain.
I give you spring fountains
You give me toxic canals.

I give you a butterfly
You give me a plastic bottle.
I give you a blackbird
You give me a stealth bomber.

I give you abundance
You give me waste.
I give you one last chance
You give me excuse after excuse.

*Roger McGough*

# Names

My name is 'Couldn't care less',
just let the forests die.
My name is 'Can't be bothered',
who cares about holes in the sky?

My name is 'I'm too busy',
let someone else do the worrying,
there's nothing that I can do
if the ice caps are wearing thin.

My name is 'Leave me alone',
just don't go preaching to me.
Gossip is what I care about
not oil that's spilt in the sea.

My name is 'I'm all right, Jack',
there's really no cause for alarm.
Hens are silly birds, who cares
if they suffer at the factory farm?

Who cares about global warming,
I like a spot of hot weather.
My name is 'Sit on the fence',
my name is 'All of a dither'.

So stop saying what I should think,
I don't want to believe what I'm told.
My name is 'Hope it will go away',
My name is 'Don't get involved'.

And who do you think you are,
telling us all we should worry?
WELL MY NAME'S A WARNING FROM FUTURE
  YEARS,
IT'S 'LISTEN OR YOU'LL BE SORRY'.

*Brian Moses*

## What Will You Do?

'What will you do to save us?'
Murmured the rustling trees.
'What will you do when the chainsaws
Buzz on the smoky breeze?'

'What will you do to save us?'
Grumbled the emerald lands.
'What will you do when the deserts
Stretch out their thirsty sands?'

'What will you do to save us?'
Pleaded the glittering snows.
'What will you do when the icebergs
Melt in a sea of woes?'

'What will you do to save us?'
Whispered the wandering streams.
'What will you do when the fishes
Vanish like stolen dreams?'

'What will you do to save us?'
Whimpered the beasts and the birds.
'What will you do when your leaders
Hush you with hollow words?'

'What is the price of a tiger?
What is a butterfly worth?
And what will you do to save them?'
Wondered the sorrowful Earth.

*Clare Bevan*

## Where Is the Forest?

Where is the forest?
cried the animals.
Where are the trees?

We needed the wood,
said the people.
Wood to make fires.
Wood to build houses.
We cut it down.

Where is the forest?
cried the animals.
Where are the trees?

We needed the land.
said the people.
Land for our cattle.
Land for our roads.
We cut it down.

Where is the forest?
cried the animals.
Where is our home?

Gone, whispered the wind.
Gone. Gone. Gone.

*John Foster*

## Our Tree

It takes so long for a tree to grow
So many years of pushing the sky.

Long branches stretch the arms
Reach out with their wooden fingers.

Years drift by, fall like leaves
From green to yellow then back to green.

Since my grandad was a boy
And then before his father's father

246

There's been an elm outside our school
Its shadow long across our playground.

Today three men ripped it down.
Chopped it up. It took ten minutes.

*David Harmer*

## *Boscastle, 2004*
### *Or: After The Flood*

The fisherman gazed across a grey sea
While his boat sloshed and rolled
On the summer waves.
No one else was about,
Only a yellow helicopter
That buzzed and hovered over his head
Like a hunting wasp.

Then he saw it,
The line of lost cars
Wandering towards him
On the puzzled tide.

He rubbed his stinging eyes,
Blinked, shook his wet hair.
He had been out too long,
That was all.
Dazed by the rain,
Or dazzled.

Yet still it came,
The strange procession –
Crazy as a daydream,
Flickery as an old film.

First, a ghostly green van
Driverless and silent
On the watery road.
Next, a small yellow racer,
Lights aglow
Windscreen bright with hope.
Now, a sleek, silver beast
Leading a caravan as clean
As a brand-new ark.

Like a flock of metal sheep
The queue bobbed patiently by,
And the fisherman watched as
Two by two
The brave survivors vanished
Between the sea-mist
And the story-book horizon.

But sometimes, when he dozes
On rainy days,
He sees them sailing on, on,
Towards the surprised
And sunlit morning
When they trundle safely home

With palm leaves under their wipers,
And their rear seats laden
With scarlet flowers.

*Clare Bevan*

## All Things Dry and Dusty

All things dry and dusty,
All plants shrivelled and small,
All trees bare and blighted,
It's man who made them all.

The shoots that twist and wither,
The rotten leaves that fall,
The fruits that do not ripen,
It's man who made them all.

All things dry and dusty,
All plants shrivelled and small,
All trees bare and blighted,
It's man who made them all.

The fields that yield no harvest,
The empty market stall,
The orchard's fruitless trees,
It's man who made them all.

All things dry and dusty,
All plants shrivelled and small,
All trees bare and blighted,
It's man who made them all.

*John Foster*

## All Things Bright and Beautiful

*Chorus:*
*All things bright and beautiful,*
*all creatures great and small,*
*all things wise and wonderful,*
*the Lord God made them all.*

Each little flower that opens,
each little bird that sings,
he made their glowing colours,
he made their tiny wings.
*Chorus*

The purple-headed mountain,
the river running by,
the sunset, and the morning
that brightens up the sky.
*Chorus*

The cold wind in the winter,
the pleasant summer sun,
the ripe fruits in the garden,
he made them every one.
*Chorus*

He gave us eyes to see them,
and lips that we might tell
how great is God Almighty,
who has made all things well.
*Chorus*

*Cecil Frances Alexander*

## There Are Too Many . . .

There are too many cats in this book.
There are too many cats in this garden, say I.
There are too many cats, says the dog,
We will get rid of them.
And the bird fluttering from the ground says 'Yes and you
   too'.
There are too many dogs in this town, agreed the cleaners.
Get rid of them and their muck and their unhealthy ways.

And the pale lettuces bemoan the slugs
And the snails the many boots that crush them regardless
   of their beauty.

251

There are too many pigeons, say the owners of pea-fields
Too many hungry sharp beaks,
say the soft-curled caterpillars.

And insects, oh insects, say the people swatting the flies,
Picking spiders out of their baths,
What need for so *many* too many? Get rid of them.

There are too many people says the earth
Too many of them dumping great loads on me
Weighing me down, covering me up, erasing my creatures.
I think I will give an extra strong shrug and heave them
   off,
These noisy squabblers, these tinkerers and complainers.
I will get rid of these far too many people
So I can breathe again.

*Jenny Joseph*

## The Lost Angels

In a fish tank in France
we discovered the lost angels,
fallen from heaven and floating now
on imaginary tides.
And all along the sides of the tank,
faces peered, leered at them,
laughing, pouting,

pointing, shouting,
while hung above their heads, a sign,
'*Ne pas plonger les mains dans le bassin*',
Don't put your hands in the tank
– the turtles bite seriously.
And who can blame them,
these creatures with angels' wings,
drifting past like alien craft.
Who knows what signals they send
through an imitation ocean,
out of sight of sky,
out of touch with stars?

Dream on, lost angels,
then one day, one glorious day,
you'll flap your wings
and fly again.

*Brian Moses*

## Menagerie

One red robin in a tree
Two swift swallows flying free
Three black badgers in a sett
Four fleet foxes running yet
Five sleek fishes diving deep
Six soft squirrels fast asleep

253

Seven wet otters in the stream
Eight kingfishers eyes agleam
Nine proud eagles sharp of sight
Ten dark barn owls in the night
Crowds of creatures low and high
Enriching sea and earth and sky.

*Stephen Bowkett*


## The Wheel Around the World

If all the world's children
wanted to play holding hands
they could happily make
a wheel around the sea.

If all the world's children
wanted to play holding hands
they could be sailors
and build a bridge across the seas.

What a beautiful chorus we would make
singing around the earth
if all the humans in the world
wanted to dance holding hands!

*Traditional from Mozambique*

## Invisible Magicians

Thanks be to all magicians.
The ones we never see,
Who toil away both night and day
Weaving spells for you and me.

The ones who paint the rainbows
The ones who salt the seas
The ones who purify the dew
And freshen up the breeze

The ones who brighten lightning
The ones who whiten snow
The ones who shine the sunshine
And give the moon its glow

The ones who buff the fluffy clouds
And powder blue the skies
The ones who splash the colours on
The sunset and sunrise

The ones who light volcanoes
The ones who soak the showers
The ones who wave the waves
And open up the flowers

The ones who spring the spring
And warm the summer air
The ones who carpet autumn
And frost the winter earth

255

The ones who polish icicles
The ones who scatter stars
The ones who cast their magic spells
Upon this world of ours

Thanks to one and thanks to all
Invisible and true
Nature's magic – heaven sent
To earth for me and you.

*Paul Cookson*

## All We Need

Food in our bellies
Hats on our heads
Water to quench us
Sheets on our beds

Teachers to teach us
Shoes on our feet
Trousers and T-shirts
Shelter and heat,

Someone to love us
Someone to love
Hope for the future
Light from above.

*Steve Turner*

256

# Big Mother

They don't come much more wild than me
and yet my child, we're family
but what I really ought to do
is introduce myself to you

I'm a gardener, that's my role
weeds to woods, I grow them all
celebrating every season
that's my life, my way, my reason

Listen now – beneath the ground:
hear that gentle, rumbling sound?
there, that's me: I'm waiting, humming
my big summer gig is coming!

Love the damp, the dark, the night
love the wind, the heat, the light
but need the rain and need the sun –
help me grow up big and strong

Cut me down and I'll be back
crawling out through every crack
first a little dandelion
next a forest – I ain't lyin':

When I say I can't be tamed
I'm always there, but rarely named
I'll always win – and that I'll wager
I'm your other Mother – Nature

*James Carter*

## A Sphere of Blue

On a sphere of blue
marbled with white
taking a trip
through silent night,

out for a spin
in starry space
go me and you
and the human race.

*Robert Hull*

## The Star

Twinkle, twinkle, little star,
How I wonder what you are!
Up above the world so high,
Like a diamond in the sky.

When the blazing sun is gone,
When he nothing shines upon,
Then you show your little light,
Twinkle, twinkle, all the night.

Then the traveller in the dark,
Thanks you for your tiny spark,
He could not see which way to go,
If you did not twinkle so.

In the dark blue sky you keep,
And often through my curtains peep,
For you never shut your eye,
Till the sun is in the sky.

As your bright and tiny spark
Lights the traveller in the dark –
Though I know not what you are,
Twinkle, twinkle, little star.

*Jane Taylor*

## First Star

Starlight, star bright,
First star that I see tonight:
From Earth, fantastically far,
I make my wishes on a star.

I wish for a world at peace
Where wars and hatred cease.
I wish for a world that's fair
Whose people give and share.
I wish for a world that's clean:
Cared for, unspoiled, green.
I wish my life to be,
With friends and family,
Loyal, loving, caring,
Adventurous and daring.

On the first star of the night,
Go wishes, go, take flight.

*Eric Finney*

## The View From Space

How beautiful Earth looks from here:
It hangs a precious, perfect sphere.
Set against vast and silent space
It seems a welcoming, warm place.

Ahead, an endless unknown story:
Star-sprinkled blackness, a cold glory.
Behind, and fading, Earth's sweet song:
There, where life is, I belong.

*Eric Finney*

# If

If you can close your eyes, and then:

see the tiger's glowing stripes
flashing in the green jungles of Bangladesh;

and hear the lonely nightingale's song
echoing in the rainbow gardens of Japan;

and taste the coconut's quenching milk,
lazing on a golden island in the Pacific;

and touch the floating iceberg's tip
creeping past the white coast of Greenland;

and scent the jasmine's delicate bloom,
strolling under the purple skies of India;

then keep travelling, friend – the world is yours.

*Debjani Chatterjee*

## If Only I Were

The chameleon wind blowing over
the rugged ranges of the Himalayas.

A tree in full regalia of autumn
on a peacock-blue lake in Vermont.

A bee upon a raft of sunlight
in the gardens of this nurturing earth.

A coral formation along the Great Barrier Reef.
The robe of the night sky filigreed with stars.

A jugalbandi raga at dawn
of sitar and shehnai, sarangi and tabla.

A wild flower greeting the weary
explorer in some forgotten desert.

A rainbow poised over the Iguacu Falls
Chanting *make me always the same as I am now*.

If only I were Mother Teresa's eyes
watching over a sick, sleeping child.

A dream come true in the warm smiles
of all the children in our world.

The healing hands of a surgeon,
   the defence of innocent folk.

The biting, trusting grip of a new-
   born child at the mother's breast.

The voices of poets, thinkers, artists, the words
   of inspiration in the struggle of our daily lives.

*Shanta Acharya*

Chameleon: tropical lizard that can change colour.
Great Barrier Reef: the largest coral reef in the world, in the Coral Sea off the coast of Australia.
Filigree: delicate ornamental work made from gold, silver or other fine twisted wire.
Jugalbandi raga: an Indian melody.
Sitar, shehnai, sarangi and tabla: Indian musical instruments.
Iguacu Falls: spectacular falls in southern Brazil, two and a half miles long and descending into the Iguacu River.
Mother Teresa: a saintly Catholic nun in Kolkata.

# *Wildlife*

Why do we say wildlife
when wildlife isn't wild?
    It's mostly soft and gentle,
    it's mostly meek and mild.
We don't see lions bombing
and tigers driving tanks,
platoons of pink flamingos
or regiments of yaks.
We don't see wars of blue whales
or rabbits flying jets,
walruses with shotguns
or parachuting pets.
To me wildlife is gentle
it loves to hide away,
it's mostly shy and silent
it likes to run and play.
    It's really us that's wildlife
    our lifestyle's really wild
    bombs
    and bangs
    and burnings
father, mother, child.

*Peter Dixon*

# *How to Explore the Universe*

Child kicks a stone –
becomes a moon.
Child kicks a spark –
becomes a star.
Child jumps the stream –
becomes a dare.
Child stares ahead –
becomes a dream.

Becomes a man.

Man sees a sky –
becomes a way.
Man makes a ship –
becomes a flight.
Man spies a light –
becomes a world.
Man walks the world –
becomes a home.
Man kicks a stone –
becomes a child.

*Stephen Bowkett*

## *A Small Star*

I live on a small star
Which it's my job to look after;
It whirls through space
Wrapped in a cloak of water.

It is a wonderful star:
Wherever you look there's life,
Though it's held at either end
In a white fist of ice.

There are creatures that move
Through air, sea and earth,
And growing things everywhere
Make beauty from dirt.

Everything is alive!
Even the stones:
Dazzling crystals grow
Deep under the ground.

And all the things belong,
Each one to the other.
I live on a precious star
Which it's my job to look after.

*Gerard Benson*

## Hurt No Living Thing

Hurt no living thing,
Ladybird nor butterfly,
Nor moth with dusty wing,
Nor cricket chirping cheerily,
Nor grasshopper, so light of leap,
Nor dancing gnat,
Nor beetle fat,
Nor harmless worms that creep.

*Christina Rossetti*

## I Am the Wizard!

I am the wizard!
Inside me float the moon and stars –
They shine as brightly as I
Make them shine.

Here within me are the seas and skies,
The fields and forests and mountains –
All of these – all! – are mine.

Somewhere nearby there lies tomorrow
Like a misty road.
Where does it go?

Anywhere I make it so.
And should I run or wander slow
It's still a road,
And by the way the grass all by itself will grow.

In my domain I am the Queen and King
And all the common kin.
And when they quarrel
So I quarrel
And where they sin
I sin.

All their yesterdays
Is my time too.
I end with them
And with them must I start.

And here at the core of our kingdom
Lies our greatest precious treasure –
Now – this moment – Now!
Measured out and made alive
By the beating of my heart.

I am my own magic,
I weave my own bright spell.
And I have learned this trick –
I listen closely when I tell.

And wonder finds me
Wherever I may seek,
For I am the wizard –
Abracadabrah!
I create life as I speak.

*Stephen Bowkett*


# He's Got the Whole World,
# in His Hand

*Chorus*:
*He's got the whole world, in His hand,*
*He's got the whole wide world, in His hand,*
*He's got the whole world, in His hand,*
*He's got the whole world in His hand.*

He's got the wind and the rain, in His hand,
He's got the wind and the rain, in His hand,
He's got the wind and the rain, in His hand,
He's got the whole world in His hand.
*Chorus*

He's got the sun and the moon, in His hand,
He's got the sun and the moon, in His hand,
He's got the sun and the moon, in His hand,
He's got the whole world in His hand.
*Chorus*

He's got the plants and the creatures, in His hand,
He's got the plants and the creatures, in His hand,
He's got the plants and the creatures, in His hand,
He's got the whole world in His hand.
*Chorus*

He's got everybody here, in His hand,
He's got everybody here, in His hand,
He's got everybody here, in His hand,
He's got the whole world in His hand.
*Chorus*

*Anon.*

## May There Be

May there be peace in the higher regions;
May there be peace in the firmament;
May there be peace on earth.
May the waters flow peacefully;
May the herbs and plants grow peacefully;
May all the divine powers bring unto us peace.
The supreme Lord is peace.
May we all be in peace, peace,
And only peace;

And may that peace
Come unto each of us.

Shanti – Shanti – Shanti

*from the Vedas*

Shanti: peace

# Celebrating
# Small Things

# To see a World in a Grain of Sand

To see a world in a grain of sand,
And a Heaven in a wild flower,
Hold infinity in the palm of your hand,
And Eternity in an hour.

*William Blake*

## The Mool Mantra
### *(The basic beliefs of Sikhs)*

There is one God,
Eternal Truth is His name,
Maker of all things
And present in all things.
Fearless and without hatred,
Timeless and formless.
Not born and not dying.
Made known by the grace of Guru Nanak.

*Traditional Sikh*

## *Praise Poem*

Let us begin
    with the hottest of days
                and the shock of icy water, sipped from
                    frosted glass.

Let us begin
    with the tickle of a ladybird
                and the rose bud of its freckled red coat.

Let us begin
    with the fizz of sherbet lemon
                sizzling on the tongue.

Let us begin
    with the sudden grin and giggle
                of a joke cracked open like a walnut.

Let us begin
    with the cat's warm purr
                and the first crazy petals of snow falling.

Let us begin
    with the kicking of legs
                as the swing flings itself higher.

Let us begin
    with a blade of grass
                and sunlight pouring through clouds like
                    golden dust.

Let us begin
   with the hot breath of chips on a cold night
               and the surprise of torchlight on a dark
                 night.

Let us begin
   by counting the rings on your fingertips
               and the mystery of a magnet's pull.

Yes, let us begin
with a few of the simple things
named Joy.

*Pie Corbett*


# Prayer to the God of All Small Things

For all the dead rabbits on the road,
Say a prayer to the god of small things.

For the limp quick fox not spry enough
To cross the glaring path;

For the dark badger coming from the quiet woods
Into the blaring night;

For the frightened deer's wood dapple leap
On to the blood red road;

For ancient toads,

For the prickled hedgehog,

For feathers stuck up from the tarmac,

For the nameless scrap of fur,

Say a prayer
To the god of all small things.

*Judith Green*


## Finding Magic

Are you looking for magic?
It's everywhere.
See how a kestrel
Hovers in air;
Watch a cat move:
What elegant grace!
See how a conker
Fits its case.
Watch a butterfly come
From a chrysalis,
Or a chick from an egg –
There's magic in this;

Then think of the
Marvellous mystery
Of an acorn becoming
A huge oak tree.
There's magic in sunsets
And patterned skies:
There's magic in moonlight –
Just use your eyes!
If you're looking for magic
It's easily found:
It's everywhere,
It's all around.

*Eric Finney*


## Joy at the Sound

Joy at the silver birch in the morning sunshine
Joy at the spring-green of its fingertips

Joy at the swirl of cold milk in the blue bowl
Joy at the blink of its bubbles

Joy at the cat revving up on the lawn
Joy at the frogs that leapfrog to freedom

Joy at the screen that fizzes to life
Joy at The Simpsons, Lisa and Bart

Joy at the dentist: 'Fine, see you next year'
Joy at the school gates: 'Closed'

Joy at the silver withholding the chocolate
Joy at the poem, two verses to go

Joy at the zing of the strings of the racquet
Joy at the bounce of the bright yellow ball

Joy at the key unlocking the door
Joy at the sound of her voice in the hall

*Roger McGough*


## Small Wonders

Brand-new elephants roamed through the jungles.
Brand-new whales splashed down through the oceans.
God had slapped them together,
Happy as a kid making mud pies.

He wiped His hands clean.
'Now for the hard part,' He thought.
He took his workbench into the garden.
Delicately He placed in the bee's sting.
The moth's antenna.

His hand
Not trembling in the slightest.

*Brian Patten*

## First and Lasting Impressions

I want to be

the first shadow dancing in the sunrise
the last negative ghost that lengthens into darkness

the first footprint crump on the blank and silent snowy
    canvas
the last drop that melts disappearing into sunlight

the first explosive splash shattering the mirrored pool
the last slowing ripple ironed into calmness

the first track followed on the ocean-swept sand
the last print washed into watery oblivion

*Paul Cookson*

## Skin Magic

That cooling hand placed on your hot brow . . .
Your toes when they're tickled by fingers . . .
When someone you love just touches your arm . . .
        Ah, skin magic
        that lingers and lingers . . .

The time when you walked hand in hand on a beach . . .
That hug when you felt, oh, so tragic . . .
The brush of lips on your tear-stained cheek . . .
  Ah, pure moments of magic,
  skin magic . . .

*Wes Magee*


## The Music I Like

The Music I like
Is very special music.

At this moment,
For instance,

I'm listening to the washing machine
Slowing down,

As the gerbil rattles
In its cage,

And my wife runs
Up the stairs

And my next door neighbour
Cuts his grass.

Music, very special music
Just listen . . .

*Ian McMillan*

## *The Fly*

How large unto the tiny fly
Must little things appear! –
A rosebud like a feather bed,
Its prickle like a spear;

A dewdrop like a looking-glass,
A hair like golden wire;
The smallest grain of mustard seed
As fierce as coals of fire;

A loaf of bread, a lofty hill;
A wasp, a cruel leopard;
And specks of salt as bright to see
As lambkins to a shepherd.

*Walter de la Mare*

## Pied Beauty

Glory be to God for dappled things –
   For skies of couple-colour as a brinded cow;
      For rose-moles all in stipple upon trout that swim;
Fresh-firecoal chestnut-falls; finches' wings;
   Landscape plotted and pieced – fold, fallow, and plough;
      And all Trades, their gear and tackle and trim.
All things counter, original, spare, strange;
   Whatever is fickle, freckled (who knows how?)
      With swift, slow; sweet, sour; adazzle, dim;
He fathers-forth whose beauty is past change:
                Praise him.

*Gerard Manley Hopkins*

## Loveliest of Trees, the Cherry Now

Loveliest of trees, the cherry now
Is hung with bloom along the bough,
And stands about the woodland ride
Wearing white for Eastertide.

Now, of my threescore years and ten,
Twenty will not come again,
And take from seventy springs a score,
It only leaves me fifty more.

And since to look at things in bloom
Fifty springs are little room,
About the woodlands I will go
To see the cherry hung with snow.

*A. E. Housman*

## Touching the Cat

Merlin's ears are as silky as rose petals.
Merlin's whiskers are as bendy as summer grass.
Merlin's fur is as cosy as a bag of hot chips.
Merlin's teeth are as spiky as cracked china.
Merlin's nose is as cool as seaside stones.
Merlin's paws are as smooth as polished conkers.
Merlin's claws are as prickly as silver pins.
Merlin's tail is as flickery as a skipping rope.
Merlin's purr is as rumbly as a whirring motor
When I touch his old, grey coat.

*Clare Bevan*

## For a Little Love

For a little love, I would go to the end of the world
I would go with my head bare and feet unshod
I would go through ice, but in my soul forever May,
I would go through the storm, but still hear the blackbird
    sing
I would go through the desert, and have pearls of dew in
    my heart.
For a little love, I would go to the end of the world,
Like the one who sings at the door and begs.

*Jaroslav Vrchlicky,*
*translated from the Czech by*
*Vera Fusek Peters and Andrew Fusek Peters*

## Hindu Poem

Sky so bright
Blue and light
Stars – how many have you?
Countless stars
Countless times
Shall our God be praised now.
Forest green
Cool, serene,
Leaves – how many have you?

Countless leaves
Countless times
Shall our God be praised now.

*Anon.*

# No One Can Call Me

Here is my heaven – on the top of a bus.
I gaze down on the no-time world.
People hurry along pavements:
women with shopping-bags and children;
men with brief-cases.
No time to look at one another
because their eyes are on the clock.
No clock to see but they feel it,
feel its hands pulling them along
away from now,
pulling them away from themselves,
making their minds its mainspring.

Here, up a stairway out of time,
I am my real self in a real world.
No one can call me, catch me –
I am not there.
Ideas are stirring underground
pushing up green shoots into the sun –
I'm wrapped in sun in this plate-glass corner.

287

There are three of us
travelling alone, coming back to ourselves
on the top of a double-decker bus.

*Phoebe Hesketh*

# Full

The day's
as full of possibilities
as of light.

Sun high already
cutting the mist apart
under shadowed trees.

*Rupert M. Loydell*

# Dream Eclipses Reality

Yesterday I painted
Great big happy faces
On all the skyscrapers
In the Gorbals . . .
And what if skyscrapers

Really did scrape
The sky?
I would attach paintbrushes
Dripping with rainbow colours
To their radio masts
And lightning conductors.

*Dee Rimbaud*

## Lizzie's Road

Little Lizzie drew a long, long road
That curled across the paper like a strange, exotic snake.
She decorated it in darkest reds and brightest blues,
Gleaming golds and glittering greens.
Mum asked, 'Why all these wonderful colours?'
'These are the rubies and emeralds and pearls,' Lizzie
    explained.
'The diamonds and opals and precious stones.'
'What a wonderful road,' said Mum. 'Is it magic?'
'No,' explained the child. 'It's just a jewel carriageway.'

*Gervase Phinn*

## Kelly Jane Dancing

When I'm dancing
when I'm dancing
my hair flies around
and I feel the rhythm thumping
to my feet on the ground.
I feel my heart speeding
and my eyes flashing clear –
my body's alive
when I'm dancing.

*Fred Sedgwick*

## Everyone Sang

Everyone suddenly burst out singing;
And I was filled with such delight
As prisoned birds must find in freedom,
Winging wildly across the white
Orchards and dark green fields; on – on – and out of sight.

Everyone's voice was suddenly lifted;
And beauty came like the setting sun:
My heart was shaken with tears; and horror
Drifted away . . . O, but Everyone
Was a bird; and the song was wordless; the singing will
    never be done.

*Siegfried Sassoon*

290

## The Spoon Music Man

My uncle
made music with spoons.

He could play
any number of tunes.

He banged them
on knees and his nose.

He banged them
on elbows and toes.

My uncle
made wonderful tunes.

He made
magical music with spoons.

*Wes Magee*

## My Fifth Birthday

On that morning,
I ran downstairs with a feeling of
WHOOSH!

For there,
In front of the French windows,
Was a two-wheeled, bright orange
Bicycle.

Throughout the day I rode it,
And the air soaked my body.

*Jonathan Malthus*

## The Power of Love

It can alter things;
The stormy scowl can become
Suddenly a smile.

The knuckly bunched fist
May open like a flower,
Tender a caress.

Beneath its bright warmth
Black ice of suspicion melts;
Danger is dazzled.

A plain and dull face
Astounds with its radiance
And sudden beauty.

Ordinary things –
Teacups, spoons and sugar-lumps –
Become magical.

The locked door opens;
Inside are leaves and moonlight;
You are welcomed in.

Its delicate strength
Can lift the heaviest heart
And snap hostile steel.

It gives eloquence
To the dumb tongue, makes plain speech
Blaze like poetry.

*Vernon Scannell*

## The Day's Eye

The sun glares,
stares down,
like a sullen eye.
Clouds frown.

The sun sleeps,
creeps into cool shade,
like a honey cat.
Shadows fade.

The sun gleams,
beams kindly heat
like an oven's plate.
Streets sweat.

The sun simmers,
glimmers bright gold,
like an old button.
Bold heat scalds.

The sun sneaks,
peeks through quiet mist,
like a sly thief.
Sunbeams fist

a hole in the cloud,
a shaft of odd light,
like a soft message
from God.

*Pie Corbett*

## The Magic of the Brain

Such a sight I saw:
An eight-sided kite surging up into a cloud
Its eight tails streaming out as if they were one.
It lifted my heart as starlight lifts the head
Such a sight I saw.

And such a sound I heard:
One bird through dim winter light as the day was closing
Poured out a song suddenly from an empty tree.
It cleared my head as water refreshes the skin
Such a sound I heard.

Such a smell I smelled:
A mixture of roses and coffee, of green leaf and warmth.
It took me to gardens and summer and cities abroad,
Memories of meetings as if my past friends were here
Such a smell I smelled.

Such soft fur I felt:
It wrapped me around, soothing my winter-cracked skin,
Not gritty or stringy or sweaty but silkily warm
As my animal slept on my lap, and we both breathed
    content
Such soft fur I felt.

Such food I tasted:
Smooth-on-tongue soup, and juicy crackling of meat,
Greens like fresh fields, sweet-on-your-palate peas,
Jellies and puddings and fragrance of fruit they are made
    from
Such good food I tasted.

Such a world comes in:
Far world of the sky to breathe in through your nose
Near world you feel underfoot as you walk on the land.
Through your eyes and your ears and your mouth
    and your brilliant brain
Such a world comes in.

*Jenny Joseph*

# Painted Petals

Toblerone-shaped yellow seeds
curved round a glow worm of lime.
Butterfly wings spread
from pink to red
like watercolours running
into space.

Strawberry and raspberry star shapes
cling to custard
and peach petals.

Branches lead
from a mustard sun.

Overlapping leaves protect
the forest flowers.

Clear crinkled skin
like seaweed veins
sliding to the centre
of the painted path,
shading the blooms.

Octopus's tentacles
bend upwards.
Hairs like fine dust
flow along the stalk.

Spindly dry roots
push through delicate winding roads.

Red and gold,
cold Indian pot,
hard against my warm hands.

The scent reaches up to Heaven,
reminds me of Spring.

Primula thinks it's Queen.

*Daisy Corbett, aged 6*

## Camden Haiku

A sudden gust –
and cherry blossom
melts on your skin.

*Ranjit Babboolal*

## Scrunch

I am not a vandal,
Nor a hooligan,
No thug at heart,
But I do love kicking leaves.

*Tony Bower*

## Catching October Leaves

Fragments of fire
Twist and twirl
Like swirls of smoke.

Scraps of flames
Spin and spiral
Tumble back to the earth.

298

They burn my feet as I kick and crunch
Through a bonfire of yellows, oranges, reds.

I scoop them up
In fiery armfuls
Fling them high into the air

Watch them float
Like burning feathers
Back into my outstretched hand.

*David Harmer*

## Southerly

This is the wind that kites the birds
and snaps the strings;
that twangs a harp of telephone wires
and tugs at gutters and eaves;
kicks timpani tins down hurrying streets,
then tries on hats that never fit
and frisbees them away.

It billows the ancient cloth of the sky
and changes the order of stars;
it tousles the heads of adventurous trees
that pull at the anxious earth.
Even the very rocks leap up

and somersault through the grass.

Oh, slam your doors if you must, my friends,
and close your windows fast –
I'm going out to find the wind
and ask where it blew my heart.

*Anne Bell*


## Floodwaters

A swarm of swifts
Sharp as knives, slice up the sky
And two herons lumber
On heavy wings over the tree-line.

Wood pigeons crash
Into the pines and sycamores
Like overweight acrobats
On a broken trapeze.

Just then a fox
Burrows into the bushes
Beside the road
The russet brush
Dragging behind him.

It took two minutes
To see these things, imagine
Spending a day there.

The branches sticking out of the water
Like dead men's fingers
The sky and the land
Bursting with wonders.

Just imagine taking the time
To look and listen
In one long moment
Just there
Down by the water.

*David Harmer*


## What I Like About Ice

The slip and slide and sheen of it,
The dizzy dance-routine of it,
The gleam and glide and glitz of it,
The pointy splintered bits of it,
The glint and gloss and glaze of it,
The crazy-paved parquets of it,
The silly fun-house floors of it,
The icicle-cold claws of it,
The whoosh and swish and shush of it,
The churning into mush of it,
The creak and crack and crunch of it,
The drinks that clink at lunch with it!

*Sue Cowling*

## The Rich Eat Three Full Meals

The rich eat three full meals, the poor two small bowls,
But peace is what matters.
Thirsty, I drink sweet plum tea;
Warm, I lie in the shade, in the breeze;
My paintings are mountains and rivers all around me,
My damask, embroidered, the grass.
I rest at night, rest easy,
Am awake with the sun
And enjoying Heaven's heaped-up favours.

*Nguyen Binh Khiem (Vietnam)*

## Miracle

In June after a brief shower
an astounding appearance of little green frogs
as if a miracle had happened,
and they had fallen down from heaven.

In March they choked the pools and ditches,
and then masses of black-centred jelly eggs
floating with moorhens and tiny water-boatmen,
speckled trout rising.

April, legions of darting tadpoles,
needle tails and bullet heads growing,
until, one evening, the cycle almost over,
first frogs leaping out
to cover the land like a plague.

The frenzied croaking died down,
they move solitary into damp garden corners,
under stones, on to reedy river banks,
juicy prey for sharp-eyed heron.

Next year, the same miracle.

*Leonard Clark*

## Fox

We've never seen a hare in Hare Way,
cats and dogs of course, the occasional horse,
but last night we saw a fox.
In the time it took to do a double take,
he'd looked at us and looked away,
he was keen to be about his business,
we were no worry to him.

In the newly darkened evening
we were pleased we'd seen
a fox with no worries
out for a stroll,
pleased our paths had crossed,
that we'd spent those briefest of seconds
watching him, watching us, watching him.

*Brian Moses*

## Glorious It Is

Glorious it is to see
The caribou flocking down from the forests
And beginning
Their wanderings to the north.
Timidly they watch
For the pitfalls of man.
Glorious it is to see
The great herds from the forests
Spreading out over plains of white.

Glorious it is to see
Early summer's short-haired caribou
Beginning to wander.
Glorious to see them trot
To and fro
Across the promontories.
Seeking for a crossing place.

304

Glorious it is
To see great musk oxen
Gathering in herds.
The little dogs they watch for
When they gather in herds.
Glorious to see.

Glorious it is
To see the long-haired winter caribou
Returning to the forests.
Fearfully they watch
For the little people,
While the herd follows the ebb-mark of the sea
With a storm of clattering hooves.
Glorious it is
When wandering time is come.

*Traditional Inuit*

# A Nest Full of Stars

Only chance made me come and find
my hen, stepping from her hidden
nest, in our kitchen garden.

In her clever secret place, her tenth
egg, still warm, had just been dropped.

Not sure of what to do, I picked up
every egg, counting them, then put them
down again. *All were mine.*

All swept me away and back.
I blinked, I saw: a whole hand
of ripe bananas, nesting.

I blinked, I saw: a basketful
of ripe oranges, nesting.

I blinked, I saw: a trayful
of ripe naseberries, nesting.

I blinked, I saw: an open bagful
of ripe mangoes, nesting.

I blinked, I saw:
a mighty nest full of stars.

*James Berry*

# The Shell

On the shelf in my bedroom stands a shell.
If I hold it close, I can smell
The salty sea.

I can hear the slap
Of the waves as they lap
The sandy shore.
I can feel once more
The tickling tide
As it gently flows
Between my toes.

*John Foster*

## Silent Song

I find
A small, white egg
Under the conker tree
In the corner of the school field

I hold
The small, white egg
In the palm of my hand
And look up into the tangled branches

The tree
Is empty and the
Small, white egg
Is cold

I think
There is a song inside
The small, white egg
That we will never hear

*Roger Stevens*


# The Pebble

One safe, summer day,
When Mum smiled,
And the sand tickled,
And even the sea-winds were gentle,
I found my magic pebble.

Now, I keep it in my blazer pocket,
So I can feel its smoothness
Under my shaking fingers
Whenever the playground roars
Like a storm,
Whenever the children screech
Like swooping gulls,
Whenever fear crashes over me
Like a freezing wave.

Then whoosh!
There is salt on my lips
As my pebble skims me away

To tickly sands,
To gentle winds,
And a safe, summer day.

*Clare Bevan*


## Stone

Hello, old friend
It's good to see you beaming
Bright and fresh faced
Moving through the evening's dreaming

And when I see you newborn
I make a wish
Just like my mother told me to
It's silly, isn't it?
Why would a wish come true?

But when I look up at the clear night sky
And try to count the stars
And feel so overwhelmed
Making a wish is somehow
Not so odd
It's as though you were
A stepping stone to God

*Roger Stevens*

## The First Bit

I love the first bit of the morning,
The bit of the day that no one has used yet,
The part that is so clean
You must wipe your feet before you walk out into it.
The bit that smells like rose petals and cut grass
And dampens your clothes with dew.

If you go out, you will bump into secrets,
Discover miracles usually covered by bus fumes.
You will hear pure echoes, whispers and scuttling.

I love the first bit of the morning
When the sun has only one eye open
And the day is like a clean shirt,
Uncreased and ready to put on;
The part that gets your attention
By being so quiet.

*Coral Rumble*

## New Day

The day is so new
you can hear it yawning,
listen:

310

The new day
is yawning
and stretching

and waiting to start.

In the clear blue sky
I hear the new day's heart.

*Ian McMillan*


## The Beauty of It

I have often wondered
     about the beauty of its

                           darkness
tall
short
at ninety degrees angle

                   to my right
                   left
                   at my rear,
                   (keeping watch)
                   in front,
                   (running away)
with the sun as its lover
I have often wondered
     about the beauty of its

                           darkness,
my Shadow.

*Don L. Lee*

## Comet-Watchers

One blind-calm summer night
someone tapped at the window of our house –
'Come out! Come out!
There's a miracle! There, in the sky!'

We jumped out of bed. What is it?
Some secret message from the stars?
I grabbed my mother's hand, it was warm,
I felt her heart beat in my palm.

Barefooted, in shirts and underpants
the whole village gathered out there in the cold;
scared old women, sleep-white faces
frozen in the white light of another world.

The poor came crowding into the street.
Women crossed their arms over their breasts.
Their knees shook as they gaped at the sky –
a fairy-tale, a holy prophecy!

Over the hill, the star-freaked sky
blazed brighter than burning hay –
a stallion with wings and a diamond mane,
a mane of fire, a streaming tail of blood.

I gripped my mother's hand like roots.
I remember the warmth of her body still,
and father pointing up at the horse
blazing away in the fires of its own sweat.

Proudly it flew away over the roofs.
We stood, still as gravestones in its fierce light.
The sky was much darker when it had gone.
O fate of comets, will o' the wisp, our hope!

*Ferenc Juhász*

## Night of the Meteors

night of the meteors
we come in
with aching necks

*Dee Evetts*

## In the Midnight Fountain

In the midnight fountain
moonlight crumples
to silver in my hand.

*Shy Mattherson*

313

## Red Flowers

red flowers
I saw on a silk tree
in the daytime
turn into my heart's desire
and haunt my mind at night.

*Miya Shūji*

## Son Rising

6 a.m. Over the bars
Of your cot your face
Rises like the sun.

*David Jacobs*

## Summer Afternoon

It's afternoon and here I lie
with my face turned to the sky
and watch the clouds that drift and run
(only flowers can stare at the sun).

Some things here are acting busy
they buzz and bustle and end up dizzy,
but the spinach, the flowers, the trees and I
we hold the ground and look at the sky.

But every plant, however slight,
is pushing and shoving for water and light,
each grass, lettuce, cherry, heaves,
kicking its roots and flexing its leaves.

In the whole garden there is only
one thing that's not doing, and that's me;
I'm not looking for food or safety or home
I lie on my back and dream this poem.

*Dave Calder*

## What Are Heavy?

What are heavy? Sea-sand and sorrow;
What are brief? Today and tomorrow;
What are frail? Spring blossoms and youth;
What are deep? The ocean and truth.

*Christina Rossetti*

## *The Big Things*

Early evening
I'm sitting in my favourite tree
gazing at the moon
in the pale summer sky
just thinking

Thinking about the big things:
like time
and infinity
and the cosmos
and how our little misty marble
of a planet
keeps spinning around
in that great murky soup
we call space

When Keith –
my next door neighbour –
peers over the fence
and says 'What you doin'
up there then?'

And I say
'Well, Keith – I was thinking
about the unstoppableness of time
and the smallness of me
and the wopping great bigness of space
and things.'

And Keith says 'Oh, right.'

And I jump down
from the tree
climb over the fence
and say 'Keith?
Do you ever think about time
and space and life
and what it all means and stuff?'

And Keith says 'Fancy a game of footie?

And I say 'Do you, Keith?
And do you think about
how the planets all turn together
like the cogs of a massive cosmic clock?'

And Keith says 'Look, you playing footie or what?'

And I say 'No seriously, Keith,
do you think about it?'

And Keith says 'I'll go in goal.'

And I say 'Oh . . . whatever.'

*James Carter*

# A Thing of Beauty
### from *Endymion*

A thing of beauty is a joy forever;
Its loveliness increases; it will never
Pass into nothingness; but still will keep
A bower quiet for us, and a sleep
Full of sweet dreams, and health, and quiet breathing.

*John Keats*

# The Journey –
# Growing, Changing,
# Old and New

## Eternity

He who bends to himself a joy
Does the wingèd life destroy;
But he who kisses the joy as it flies
Lives in eternity's sunrise.

*William Blake*

## A Prayer for Travellers

May the road rise up to meet you.
May the wind always be at your back.
May the sun shine warm upon your face,
the rains fall soft upon your fields and,
until we meet again,
may God hold you in the palm of his hand.

*Irish blessing*

## Barnsley to Bethlehem

'Are we nearly at Bethlehem?'
asked my son.

'We're going to Barnsley!' was my reply.

321

Funny thing
confusing Barnsley with Bethlehem.
The wise men got it right,
no confusion there.

Funny thing is
you can find Jesus in Barnsley
as well as in Bethlehem.
You can find him anywhere
if you're looking.

*Tony Bower*

## Journey Home

I remember the long homeward ride, begun
By the light that slanted in from the level sun;
And on the far embankment, in sunny heat,
Our whole train's shadow travelling, dark and complete.

A farmer snored. Two loud gentlemen spoke
Of the cricket and news. The pink baby awoke
And gurgled awhile. Till slowly out of the day
The last light sank in glimmer and ashy-grey.

I remember it all; and dimly remember, too,
The place where we changed – the dark trains lumbering
    through;

The refreshment-room, the crumbs and the slopped tea;
And the salt on my face, not of tears, not tears, but the
    sea.

Our train at last! Said Father, 'Now tumble in!
It's the last lap home!' And I wondered what 'lap' could
    mean;
But the rest is all lost, for a huge drowsiness crept
Like a yawn upon me; I leant against Mother and slept.

*John Walsh*

## The Train of the Stars

The night is a train that passes,
Up on my house I watch it
Its eyes smile to me.

The night is a train that passes,
Carrying moons and stars,
Clouds, flowers,
Seas and rivers that run.
The night is a train that passes.

The night is a train that passes,
I wish, oh, how I wish!
I could take it one day:
It would take me away,
To see where it's going.
Oh, where's that train going?


*Abdul-Raheem Saleh al-Raheem,*
*translated by Adil Saleh Abid*


## Road

*'. . . happiness isn't on the road to anything . . . happiness*
  *is the road'*
          *(Bob Dylan, quoting his maternal grandmother)*

Put your ear
against this road
and you will hear
the wheels that rolled

The souls that passed
the stories told
of journeys made
from young to old

The towns that rose
the dreams that fell
the weary resting
by the well

The hopeful going
back for more
the soldier coming
home from war

The horses' hooves
the driving rain
the travellers' tales
the circus train

The songs the cries
the laughs the lies
the lovers lost in
long goodbyes

And though this road
will let you roam
it's always there
to take you home

*James Carter*

## Setting Off

Holidays begin with
Tea, toast
And darkness.
Mum whispers,
'Quietly now, or you'll wake the neighbours.'
Like escaping prisoners we tiptoe towards the car
Where pillows and blankets wait silently on the back seats.

The car engine explodes into life
And we slide out into a night that belongs
To cats
And milkmen,
Where the road's black tongue
Slips beneath our wheels
And licks its lips.

*John Coldwell*

## Getting There

Call for a taxi, Maxie,
Or phone for a mini-cab;
Don't worry about the meter,
I'll gladly pick up the tab.

Ignore the doorman, Norman,
The cabbies are all on strike;
It's got to be Shanks's Pony,
Or getting on your bike.

Jump on the ferry, Jerry,
It sails on the morning tide;
All day the bars will stay open
On the port (and the sherry) side.

Leap on your cycle, Michael,
And zoom very fast, then display
The proper hand-signal for Norman,
Should you happen to meet on the way.

On to your scooter, Pooter,
As pompous as pompous can be;
The tin-tacks we've spread out will puncture
Your tyres and your vanity.

Into your Morris, Doris;
I wish I'd been given the chance
To join you; we'd park and together
Alight for a quick Morris dance.

Drive the jalopy, Poppy;
It's ancient but none of us care
How bumpy and lengthy the journey
As long as we get safely there.

*Vernon Scannell*

## Childhood Tracks

Eating crisp fried fish with plain bread.
Eating sheared ice made into 'snowball'
with syrup in a glass.
Eating young jelly-coconut, mixed
with village-made wet sugar.
Drinking cool water from a calabash gourd
on worked land in the hills.

Smelling a patch of fermenting pineapples
in stillness of hot sunlight.
Smelling mixed whiffs of fish, mango, coffee,
mint, hanging in a market.
Smelling sweaty padding lifted off a donkey's back.

Hearing a nightingale in song
in moonlight and sea-sound.
Hearing dawn-crowing of cocks, in answer
to others around the village.
Hearing the laughter
of barefeet children carrying water.
Hearing a distant braying of a donkey
in a silent hot afternoon.
Hearing palmtrees' leaves rattle
on and on at Christmas time.

Seeing a woman walking in loose floral frock.
Seeing a village workman with bag and machete
under a tree, resting, sweat-washed.
Seeing a tangled land-piece of banana trees
with goats in shades cud-chewing
Seeing a coil of plaited tobacco
like rope, sold, going in bits.
Seeing children playing in schoolyard
between palm and almond trees.
Seeing children toy-making in a yard
while slants of evening sunlight slowly disappear.
Seeing an evening's dusky hour lit up
by dotted lamplight.
Seeing fishing nets repaired between canoes.

*James Berry*

## Magic Wand

My baby brother was born
With a broken heart.
He spent his entire tiny life
In the whispering ward
Where the doctors did their best to mend him
With their tubes and their stitches
And their beeping machines.
But sometimes science
Isn't as clever as it seems.

And Dad said
What we really needed
Was for someone to invent
A magic wand.

My baby brother isn't sick any more.
He is tucked up cosily
In a small white box
Covered with a rainbow of flowers.
Mum says his face
Is as peaceful and perfect
As a brand-new doll,
But now our whole family
Has a broken heart.
And I wish
I wish
Someone would suddenly invent
That magic wand.

*Clare Bevan*

## Meet Me Anywhere

Meet me,
      Anywhere, anywhere
         anywhere

Where you head-butt the ball so hard
the goalie stands no chance
where you ride the bicycle so well
you can let go the use of your hands

Where your grandmother piles your plate so high
it's as if it is her stomach she's filling
where your mother chases you round the front room
to rub cocoa butter on your dry skin

      Meet me anywhere

The sky wants you under it
With secrets for you to find
God will tickle you even as you sleep
That's why some days you wake up smiling

But even in a hurricane
You can . . .

     Whisper, whistle, pull, push,
       shout, cry, smile, laugh

I'll find you
and I'll meet you anywhere

It is as if
tears that rolled around the sun
flushed through my heart
and burst through my eyes
at your first breath.

And the feel of your tiny hands
wrapped around one of my fingers
has made more a man of me
than I could ever make of myself.

It is as if
smiles that were smuggled out of pain
came by to give you dimples
and seeing you
at your mother's breast
makes me search my soul
for all that I can give you

And I will meet you anywhere
give you my everything

Anywhere

*Abraham Gibson*

## New Baby

So there she was, my dark-eyed new sister,
Only a few hours old, sleeping by mother,
I bent over her cot and most gently kissed her,
Feeling so glad that I was her brother.

She looked very tiny, her face rather wrinkled,
With mother soft-smiling that we were together,
Her hair black and shining, her baby hands crinkled,
Born early that evening in cold winter weather.

I gave the glad news to my dogs and my tabby cat,
Then went to bed to a night of light dreaming,
Of Ugandan elephants, tigers in Gujerat,
And the sun on their rivers for ever bright gleaming.

But most of my sister, with the sandalwood smelling
Sweetening the air of our small English dwelling.

*Leonard Clark*

## *Dedicating a Baby*
### *(from the Pygmy tradition)*

Life is a tree – rooted in the earth,
An old tree – our family tree.

God planted the tree –
He makes it grow
Strong roots,
Wide branches.

And now we bring this baby,
A bud on the great tree

All life is God's life
And the life in this baby is God's life.

We – the roots and branches of the ancient tree
Offer this new bud baby to our Creator God.

Together we will grow.

*Jan Dean*

# First Thing Today
### for Jimmy

First thing today before
the cockerel crowed –
a baby's cry from
across the road.

Hi there, baby,
damp and furled,
hi there. Welcome
to our world.

Here's the little finger
of my right hand
and here's a teddy
you won't understand

                                          yet

                                                  and

here's

flowers for your mummy
and what about this? –
Here's my first hug
and my first kiss.

*Fred Sedgwick*

## Looking Forward

The days are getting longer.
From my first-floor window
I can sit and watch
the tide of people ebb and flow.
I know them all
the early-morning milkman
postman
paperboy
the schoolchild
worker
shopper.
I invent their lives.
Now I have started looking forward
to the sights and sounds
of summer evenings
by my open window
children playing late
lawnmowers
couples walking dogs.
And yet
perhaps this summer I shall not be here.
My days are getting shorter.

*Sue Cowling*

## The Funeral

Everyone is silent in the huge black car.
A cloud full of swallowed tears
gliding two feet above the ground
towards a storm.

We're trying to be brave.
Mum holds my hand tightly.
Her fingers are like clothes pegs
clinging to washing
in a force 9 gale.
'You're hurting me,' I say.
She lets me go –
a forgotten balloon
and smiles a smile from far away,
like a smile in a photograph
in a place you can't quite remember.

We wait in line.
People mumble past us
trying not to catch our eyes.
I look at the coffin
and try to imagine Granny inside.
Can she hear me singing?
I'm singing really loudly so she'll hear.

Is she in heaven yet?
Still old and in pain?

Or whirring swiftly backwards
like a rewound tape
which pauses
at your very favourite bit.

Are hosts of heavenly angels
even as we sing
loosening her tight grey perm
and itchy curls?
Making the hair flow
like a coppery stream
down her strong young back.

I wonder if she'll wear
her tartan slippers
to dance on the clouds.

Afterwards, outside,
we weave through furious rain
towards the car.
Inside and warm again,
Mum sighs
Like summer
drifting through an open window
A feather
              or a present
                            from a sky-blue
                                          sky.

*Lindsay MacRae*

## Hospice

Nice word, 'Hospice'.
Sort of tickle-the-lip
make-you-smile
kind of word.

Auntie Win is in a hospice
sleepy head
cosy bed
friends and flowers
comfy hours.

She says it is a happy place.
'Hospice',
sort of tickles the lip.
I expect that's why she smiles a lot.

*Peter Dixon*

## Losing at Home

I never really cried when my grandma died.
You see I was away from home at the time.
The first time I saw my grandfather afterwards
he was watching World Cup football on the telly.

He told me that it was a good match and that
the goalkeeper had made some fantastic saves
although we were still one nil down.
But somewhere behind his eyes
a light had dimmed
and on the other side of his glasses
I could see teardrops forming
and as they fell down his face
they weren't because his team had lost
but because he had lost
his team.

You see, to my grandfather
my grandmother was his best team
in the world.
Ever.

*Paul Cookson*

## Nan's Song

I was so busy, I didn't see
the first green leaves on the willow tree.
I'll save my time, in future springs,
for all the most important things.

*Anne Bell*

## Trails

I once walked along the trails of my ancestors
through deserts, mountains, rivers and sands
where food was plenty,
where goanna tracks led to waterholes
where the bandicoot whistled its name.
I gathered nuts from the kurrajong tree
and suckled wild honey.
I swam with catfish in billabongs of waterlilies
and tasted cooked food from ovens underground.
I smelled the promise of the winds
along trails of the dreaming
and traced my mother's footsteps embedded in the sand.
I once walked along the trails of my ancestors
that now have blown away with the winds of time.
Only in memory will I walk along the trails
Only in memory will they remain.

*Eva Johnson*

## Shelley

I was thinking about my dog,
Shelley.
She died a while ago
but you still remember friends, don't you,
friends who have passed away.

She was unhappy at the end,
confused, she would bump into
the furniture, and stand
staring into the corner of the room.
But I was thinking about the good times.
When she leapt into the icy water
at Betws-y-coed
and had to be rescued.
She loved swimming in the sea
and shaking herself dry over sunbathers,
especially old wrinkly ones.
She was a great one for fetching
sticks and balls –
you couldn't take her to tennis matches.
You know, sometimes I think I hear her
in the next room.
I forget she's gone,
Just the wind, I suppose,
rippling through my memories.

*Roger Stevens*

## Grandad

*Grandad's dead
And I'm sorry about that.*

He'd a huge black overcoat.
He felt proud in it.
You could have hidden
A football crowd in it.
Far too big –
It was a lousy fit
But Grandad didn't
Mind a bit.
He wore it all winter
With a squashed black hat.

*Now he's dead*
*And I'm sorry about that.*

He'd got twelve stories.
I'd heard every one of them
Hundreds of times
But that was the fun of them:
You knew what was coming
So you could join in.
He'd got big hands
And brown, grooved skin
And when he laughed
It knocked you flat.

*Now he's dead*
*And I'm sorry about that.*

*Kit Wright*

## Sensing Mother

Dad keeps Mum's favourite dress
deep in the bottom of the ottoman.
Sometimes, when he is at work
I stand listening to the tick of the clock
then go upstairs.

And propping up
the squeaky wooden lid, I dig through
layers of rough, winter blankets
feeling for that touch of silk.
The blue whisper of it cool
against my cheek.

Other times – the school-test times,
and Dad-gets-home-too-late-
to-say-goodnight times –
I wrap the arms of the dress around me,
breathing in a smell, faint as dried flowers.

I remember how she twirled around
– like a swirl of sky.

When I am old enough I will wear it.
Pulling up the white zip,
I'll laugh and spin,
calling out to my daughter:
*How do I look?*

*Mandy Coe*

344

# Death

There is no needle without piercing point.
There is no razor without trenchant blade.
Death comes to us in many forms.

With our feet we walk the goat's earth.
With our hands we touch God's sky.
Some future day in the heat of noon,
I shall be carried shoulder high
Through the village of the dead.
When I die, don't bury me under forest trees,
I fear their thorns.
When I die, don't bury me under forest trees,
I fear the dripping water.
Bury me under the great shade trees in the market,
I want to hear the drums beating
I want to feel the dancers' feet.

*Kuba (Africa)*

# Remember

Remember me when I am gone away,
    Gone far away into the silent land;
    When you can no more hold me by the hand,
Nor I half turn to go yet turning stay.

Remember me when no more day by day
    You tell me of our future that you plann'd:
    Only remember me; you understand
It will be late to counsel then or pray.
Yet if you should forget me for a while
    And afterwards remember, do not grieve:
    For if the darkness and corruption leave
    A vestige of the thoughts that once I had,
Better by far you should forget and smile
    Than that you should remember and be sad.

*Christina Rossetti*


## Tracey's Tree

Last year it was not there,
the sapling with purplish leaves
planted in our school grounds with care.
It's Tracey's tree, my friend who died,
and last year it was not there.

Tracey, the girl with long black hair
who, out playing one day, ran
across a main road for a dare.
The lorry struck her. Now a tree grows
and last year it was not there.

Through the classroom window I stare
and watch the sapling sway.
Soon its branches will stand bare.
It wears a forlorn and lonely look
and last year it was not there.

October's chill is in the air
and cold rain distorts my view.
I feel a sadness that's hard to bear.
The tree blurs, as if I've been crying
and last year it was not there.

*Wes Magee*

## The Homecoming
### for Emaia

For a moment, we burn so bright;
And then, in one cruel second,
We are gone.

While time was out
Pacing the porch,
Walking the dog up the back lane;
Grief came calling –
Left us stunned.

347

At first, we shunned the world;
The pain swallowed us quite whole;
It took its shabby toll
Upon our lives.

And waking then, we wondered, again and again,
What will become of her?
Surely she will come back –
Reborn into each sweet atom
Of the moth's dumb dance –
Or balanced on the candle's wick,
Fluid and impossibly golden.
Perhaps she will come back
As the bewildered scent of a bluebell
Or the pollen brushing a bee's leg.
Perhaps she will surprise you
In an ant's sudden tickle –
Or the fickle spider's sticky web.

Whatever happens –
She will come back
To be a part of all that delights
And surrounds you.

Tonight, as greedy grief eats
At your soul
And frightens you –
She is free enough already –
Wandering still
Where the heavy hurt heart yearns;

Where the piercing pain burns;
It seems we cannot yet shake off our grief.

Yes, life passes – too brief.
We read each other –
A library of lives
Lit by sudden loving –
Page upon page,
Age upon age,
Sweet memory laced
by sweet memory.

Graced by passing lives,
so we are lit –
And live on.

*Pie Corbett*

## Farewell

Thy journey be auspicious; may the breeze,
Gentle and soothing, fan thy cheek; may lakes
All bright with lily cups delight thine eye,
The sunbeam's heat be cooled by shady trees,
The dust beneath thy feet the pollen be
Of lotuses.

*Anon.*

## Time

Time is too slow for those who wait,
too swift for those who fear,
too long for those who grieve,
too short for those who rejoice,
but for those who love, time is eternity.

*Anon.*

## E Tipu e Rea
*an oriori (lullaby)*

| | |
|---|---|
| Moe mai rā e te hua | Sleep my loved one |
| I tō moenga pai | In your comfortable bed. |
| Kaua rā e tahuri | Don't be restless. |
| Taupoki ki roto I tō | Snuggle up safe and sound in your |
| | |
| Papanarua | Duvet so that you are warm. |
| Kia mahana ai | |
| Ka tō te marama e | When the translucent rays |
| Tiaho nei | Of the moon disappear |
| Ka hī ake ko te rā | A new day dawns with the rising |
| | |
| Kei tua o te pae | Of the sun beyond the horizon. |

350

| | |
|---|---|
| Tipu kē ake koe | So too does the cycle of life continue. |
| Me he horoeka | Grow up strong and gracious, |
| Torotika kit e rā | Just like the proud horoeka tree, |
| Whāia te Māramatanga | Confident and free. Seek out the secrets of the hidden |
| O te hinengaro O te wairua | well-spring of your mind And know the sounds and Dreams of your spirit. |
| Kia puāwai koe ki Te ao | So you shall blossom into the world, |
| Ka kitea ō painga | And the world in turn is transformed. |

*Hirini Melbourne, translated by Mere Skerrett-White*

## The Stem of the Branch

None on earth is like her,
She that made me breathe.

None on earth is like her,
She that filled my stomach.

None on earth is like her,
She that knew why I cried.

None on earth is like her,
She that protected me.

None on earth is like her,
She that gave me my first lessons.

None on earth is like her,
She whose death orphans me.

*L. M. Asiedu*

# Psalm 23
### A Psalm of David

The Lord *is* my shepherd; I shall not want.

He maketh me to lie down in green pastures: he leadeth
me beside the still waters.

He restoreth my soul: he leadeth me in the paths of
righteousness for his name's sake.

Yea, though I walk through the valley of the shadow of
death, I will fear no evil: for thou *art* with me; thy rod
and thy staff they comfort me.

Thou preparest a table before me in the presence of mine
enemies: thou anointest my head with oil; my cup runneth
over.

Surely goodness and mercy shall follow me all the days of
my life: and I will dwell in the house of the LORD for
ever.

*Psalm 23:1–6*
*King James Bible*

## I Dream of a Time

I dream of a time

When the only blades are blades of corn
When the only barrels are barrels of wine
When the only tanks are full of water
When the only chains are chains of hands

I hope for a time . . .

*John Foster*

## The Doctor

When I listened
To my enemy's heart

I recognized the same
drumbeat of dreams
that I listen to each night.

*Cally Breeze*

## Difference

As long as we see others
as different,
there will be hurt,
there will be pain,
there will be wars,
there will be more cold rain

falling

between us.

The day we learn
to shed our fear
like a snake casting its skin . . .

The day we learn
to see that we are all

moulded

from the same warm clay.

That will be the day,
when the sun
breaks through.

That will be the day,
when we first see
our true
selves.

*Pie Corbett*


## Peacekeepers

Once again the flat is cold as ash
mother's nose is pinched and pink,
her shivering hands are blue.

Our breath fumes like smokers'
as she rolls me into the blanket.
But soldiers, stamping on street corners,
are the only ones with cigarettes.

She speaks in fingers and whispers.
The blanket is warm,
but it prickles.

She carries me down,
leaves me under the stairs,
goes to join food queues.

I wait, sometimes till dim light darkens,
watching the spider on her ropes.
When footsteps shake walls
she knots tight to a corner.

I mustn't cry out
otherwise more windows will break,
more ceilings fall
and soldiers, sick of screams,
will come clubbing through the rubble,
keeping the peace.

*Chris Kinsey*

## Chantha

Chantha
Aged thirteen.
Once she made traps,
Traps in school.

Nine years old and she made traps in school
Lessons that taught her the art of war
The sharpening of bamboo
The binding together of wood
The careful assembly of pain

Traps to maim
Traps to injure
Traps to wound
Traps to puncture the skin
Traps to shed blood
But traps to protect
Traps to protect her family
Traps to protect her family from the enemy

Chantha
Aged thirteen
Now she paints pictures
Now she sings songs
Now she smiles in school
Now she doesn't make traps

Chantha
Aged thirteen
At last she understands the word *peace*
At last she chooses what she does
At last she watches her uncle's television
At last she sits openly with her family round the radio

Chantha
Aged thirteen
Has learnt how to smile
But
Chantha
Aged thirteen
Once made traps

*Paul Cookson*


## Mwajuma Wants to Return Home

Mwajuma wants to return home
But home is not a safe place to be
Home is where the war is

*Peace is my right* says Mwajuma
*Peace is our right* say her friends

Some have been child soldiers,
Kidnapped, forced to fight,
Not games to play, make believe, pretend
But real guns with real bullets.

Others have seen parents slaughtered,
Mum murdered
Dad dead
The eyes of the children

Seeing things they should never have to see,
Not even on TV.

Because of the war
Because of the death
Because of the murder
Because of the slaughter
They are angry for peace

Angry for peace

Peace is their future
And so they strive to be fishermen for peace
Casting that net of love wide
Trying to catch even a little piece of peace

Because even a little piece of peace
Is better
Than no peace at all.

*Paul Cookson*

## The Soldiers Came

The soldiers came
and dropped their bombs.
The soldiers didn't take long
to bring the forest down.

With the forest gone
the birds are gone.
With the birds gone
who will sing their song?

But the soldiers forgot
to take the forest
out of the people's hearts.
The soldiers forgot
to take the birds
out of the people's dreams.
And in the people's dreams
the birds still sing their song.

Now the children
are planting seedlings
to help the forest grow again.
they eat a simple meal of soft rice
wrapped in a banana leaf.
And the land welcomes their smiling
like a shower of rain.

*John Agard*

# Christmas 1992

Under a threadbare blanket, on a mattress of stone,
A teenager shivers, cold and alone.

High on a mountainside, on a carpet of snow,
A refugee waits with nowhere to go.

Under a blistering sky, on a cushion of sand,
A starving child squats and holds out her hand.

*John Foster*

## The Refugee's Wish

The moon belongs
up in the sky –
so too the stars –
but where do I?

The sun is safe
up in the sky –
so too the clouds –
but what of I?

Like a fallen star
or a meteorite –
lost in this place,
not feeling quite right.

Far from home
in a world adrift –
where a chance to belong
would be a gift.

*Tania Wartalski*


## Scarecrow Christmas

In winter fields
a scarecrow sings
the hopeful tune
of lonely kings.

His empty heart
is thin and cold.
his cruel rags
are worn and old.

But in our homes
we sing out clear,
warm words of joy
and know no fear.

In bed at night
we listen for
padded footsteps
at the door.

In other fields
and different lands,
living scarecrows
reach out hands.

They live beneath
the sun's cruel rays.
They do not know
of Christmas days.

*Pie Corbett*


## *Three-Minute Silence, Three-Minute Poem*

bells chime
14th September
2001

all alone in a staffroom in Barnsley
but thinking of America,
remembering New York . . .

the blur of crashing planes as missiles
falling skyscrapers
raging fire and monstrous dust clouds

and the dead
the innocent dead
the thousands of innocent dead

and still there is the disbelief
numbed with the knowledge of reality
but chilled with the disbelief

trying to believe the unbelievable
trying to think of something
just something

half-formed prayers disintegrate
and a half-formed poem
drifts off into nothingness

as bells chime
on the 14th September
2001

all alone in a staffroom in Barnsley

*Paul Cookson*

## The News

I don't like news
that explodes
leaves refugees
crying, homeless

that orders tanks
into cities
blasting down
schools and houses.

News that blows up
hospitals
news that kills
and fills deep graves.

I don't like news
that screams abuse
kicks the legs
from under wingers

taps their ankles
argues back
news that won't learn
how to lose.

I like news
that's just been born
news that puts
food in stomachs.

news that rescues
news that cures
that celebrates
its hundredth birthday

news that will make today
happier than the day before.

*David Harmer*

## A Time to Be Silent

Before the soccer game
In the stadium
We remembered the tragedy
When so many supporters died

For one minute
Fifty thousand
Men, women and children
Were silent

Even insects and birds
Seemed to sense
The moment
And were quiet

The wind held its breath
And time slowed

It was the loudest silence
I have ever heard.

*Roger Stevens*

## War Story

*Mum, I saw the news today*
*Filled with words of war,*
*People crying far away,*
*I can't understand what for?*

War is a mountain of hate,
A sad, unconquerable hill,
Why can't they share the view at the top?
But it's cold as they go for the kill . . .

*Mum, I saw the papers today*
*It said that children were dead,*
*Were they being very naughty?*
*Mum, there's a fear in my head.*

The young ones are like butterflies
For men with nets of steel,
Who've soldered up their rusting hearts,
And can no longer feel.

*Mum, I heard the radio say*
*That mothers were taken away,*
*Oh mum don't ever leave me,*
*And promise me you'll stay.*

Oh, war is a ship of stone, my girl,
Whoever's sails will sink,
A storm is raging in their hearts,
And no one stops to think
That war is a ship of stone my girl
The ocean's bitter drink;
But hold me tight my darling,
We teeter on the brink.

*Andrew Fusek Peters and Polly Peters*

## Galilee

I remember rowing
on the lake late at night –

with the town lights dancing
on the waves –

and the sweet smell
of orange blossom drifting

from the dry banks

where we stopped to see
where Jesus walked upon the water

and the hillside where he
fed the crowd bread and fishes –

and near the border
in Rosh Pinna

we sipped tea
and stared across

at the Golan Heights –

as a humming bird whirred
as it too sipped

from the beak of a scarlet flower

and today as the bombs thud
I remember that dusty land,

I remember

eating a slice of sweet watermelon
like a clown's smile

from a child's painting.

                                        *Pie Corbett*

## Boy at the Somme

'The last one there is a cow pat!'
grinned the small boy
running between the white headstones
as he began the one hundred metre dash
along the narrow strip of turf separating
Private Tom Atkins, age 18, of the Lancashire Fusiliers,
from Lieutenant Edward Hollis, age 19,
of the Seaforth Highlanders;
more than twice the distance they managed
over the same small field
that October morning eighty-seven years before
into the spitting venom of the machine guns
that killed them instantly.

*Alan Durant*

## Bethlehem

*Secrets live in the space between our footsteps.*
The words of my grandfather echoed in my dreams,
as the years kept his beads and town.
I saw Bethlehem, all in dust, an empty town
with a torn piece of newspaper lost in its narrow streets.
Where could everyone be? Graffiti and stones answered.
And where was the real Bethlehem – the one

my grandfather came from?
Handkerchiefs dried the pain from my hands.
Olive trees and tears continued to remember.
I walked the town until I reached an old Arab man
dressed in a white robe.
I stopped him and asked, 'Aren't you the man I saw in
my grandfather's stories!'
He looked at me and left. I followed him – asked him
why he left? He continued walking.
I stopped, turned around and realized he had left me
the secrets in the space between his footsteps.

*Nathalie Handal*

## from *Thread by Thread*

Thread by thread
knot by knot
like colonies of ants
we weave a bridge

Thread by thread
piece by piece
knitting embroidering
sewing decorating
thread by thread
we weave
the map of conciliation.

Rachel's is white
Yemima's purple
Amal's is green
Salima's rose-coloured
thread by thread
we stitch together
torn hearts
bind the map of conciliation.

I pray for the life of Ami and Nitsi
you pray for Ilan, Shoshi and Itsik
and she prays
for Jehan, Asheraf and Fahed
with the same tear.
Word and another word
prayer and another prayer
and our heart is one
we embroider in hope
with the sisterhood of workers
a map of love
to tear down the borders . . .

*Bracha Serri,*
*translated by Shlomit Yaacobi*
*and Nava Mizrahhi*

## Poppy Day
### Prayer of Remembrance

In the rising of the sun and in its going down, we
remember them; In the glowing of the wind and in the chill
of winter; In the opening of buds and in the rebirth of
spring; In the blueness of the sky and in the warmth of
summer; In the rustling of leaves and in the beauty of
autumn; In the beginning of the year and when it ends;
When we are weary and in the need of strength; When we
are lost and sick at heart; When we have joys we yearn to
share, we remember them. So long as we live, they too
shall live, for they are now a part of us, as we remember
them.

*Anon.*

## Behind the Scenes

I lay shivering and cold in the thick, haunted darkness
but you showed me how to sleep.
I stepped barefoot on to sharp, sheared splinters
but you crushed them beneath my feet.
I was swallowed by the hungry, greedy sea
but you pulled me to the beach.
I stretched out for blistering, glowing coals
but you blew them out of reach.

I fell like a stone from the highest mountain
but you taught me how to fly.
And when, at times, I soared in silence,
touched the heat of the sun-washed sky,
tasted the mint of morning mists
that rose above the hills and trees,
gazed down on the deserts, oceans,
smelled the sweetness of summer breeze,
I knew you were never far away . . .
watching, smiling, pleased.

*Mark Halliday*


## The Worst of Our Dreams

Funny how it seems
I can remember the worst of our dreams
whenever the Big Bad Things happen.

On a train
from the Isle of Wight
I had the fright
of my life
when the man on the seat opposite me
leant across to tell me
that the twin towers had fallen.

Funny how it seems
I can remember the worst of our dreams
whenever the Big Bad Things happen.

On Boxing Day
in Folkestone
surrounded by the crumpled skins of wrapping paper
and orange scabs of tangerine peel
watching the tsunami on TV
like a distant disaster film
but knowing this was real
as the sea punched its watery hand
and ripped up the land,
shredding lives as easily as leaves
torn apart in the breeze.

Funny how it seems
I can remember the worst of our dreams
whenever the Big Bad Things happen.

In a hotel
in Milton Keynes
with teachers on a course,
when a text message arrived to say:
'I'm OK. Don't worry. I've arrived.'
Another lucky one stumbling
like a blind mole out of the underground
covered in the dust of disaster.

Funny how it seems
I can remember the worst of our dreams
whenever the Big Bad Things happen.

And whenever the hand of grief
grabs the world in its teeth
and we are hurled
into pain beyond belief

I remember
that most of us are the lucky ones,
left covered only in the dust
and it must act as a reminder
to be kinder
while we can,
to be kinder
while we can.

*Pie Corbett*

## Comfort

Even

if

you

forget

God

–

He

Will

Never

Forget

You.

*Anon.*

## *The Prime Minister Is Ten Today*

This morning I abolished
homework, detention and dinner ladies.
I outlawed lumpy custard, school mashed spuds
and handwriting lessons.
From now on playtimes must last two hours
unless it rains, in which case we all go home
except the teachers who must do extra PE
outside in the downpour.

Whispering behind your hand in class
must happen each morning between ten and twelve,
and each child needs only do
ten minutes' work in one school hour.

I've passed a No Grumpy Teacher law
so one bad word or dismal frown
from Mr Spite or Miss Hatchetface
will get them each a month's stretch
sharpening pencils and marking books
inside the gaol of their choice.

All headteachers are forbidden
from wearing soft-soled shoes
instead they must wear wooden clogs
so you can hear them coming.
They are also banned from shouting
or spoiling our assembly by pointing
at the ones who never listen.

Finally the schools must shut
for at least half the year
and if the weather's really sunny
the teachers have to take us all
to the seaside for the day.

If you've got some good ideas
for other laws about the grown-ups
drop me a line in Downing Street
I'll always be glad to listen
come on, help me change a thing or two
before we all grow up
and get boring.

*David Harmer*

# No More

No more bombs,
No more tanks,
No more armies,
Arrayed in ranks.

No more air raids,
No more mines,
No dead bodies,
In long, sad lines.

No more ruined cities,
No fatherless child,
No frail widow,
Weeping wild.

When I have power,
There'll be no war,
But peace on Earth
For evermore –
– Just peace on Earth
For evermore.

*John Kitching*

## Now Children Rule

Children of the world,
now that we rule, we will be as one nation.

Children of the starved lands
now that we rule, we will feed you.

Mad dictators and makers of war,
now that we rule, your voices shall be ignored
and you will dwindle into nothingness . . .

Deluded priests and fanatical fools,
now that we rule, we will laugh at you
and your churches and temples will fall into dust.

Weapons of destruction,
now that we rule, you yourselves will be destroyed.

Cousins in fur and feather,
now that we rule, we shall leave space for you too.

Mighty oceans,
now that we rule, no poisons will be poured into your
vast deeps.

Wild wind,
now that we rule, no evil fumes will sully your purity.

Flowers of the field,
now that we rule, you shall pour your sweetness into the
spring air.

Great trees of the steaming jungle,
now that we rule, your green canopy will spread to
protect the world.

Grown-ups,
now that we rule, you will behave yourselves.

*Marian Swinger*

## The Minister of Awe and Wonder

To watch the sun rise every morn,
To hear the sounds of breaking dawn.
To marvel at new buds that grow
Through frosted ground and soil below.
To catch the first drop of rain in May
To stop and ponder every day.
To celebrate each storm and thunder
For I am the Minister of Awe and Wonder.

To view the gold of Autumn leaves
To speculate how rivers freeze.
To watch a spider spin its web
With filaments of silken thread.
To stare and gaze with fresh surprise
To view the world with child's eyes.
Admire, respect but never plunder
So says the Minister of Awe and Wonder.

*Chris Ogden*

# Signs, Stories
and Symbols

Bring me the sunset in a cup

*Emily Dickinson*

When winds take forests in their paws
The universe is still.

*Emily Dickinson*

## Beauty

He who meets beauty and does not look at it will soon be
poor:
Red feathers are the pride of the parrot,
Young leaves are the pride of the palm-tree,
White flowers are the pride of the leaves,
A well-swept verandah is the pride of the householder,
A straight tree is the pride of the forest,
The fast deer is the pride of the bush,
The rainbow is the pride of heaven,
A beautiful woman is the pride of her husband,

Children are the pride of their mother,
The moon and stars are the pride of the sun,
Beauty and good luck are on their way!

*Traditional Yoruba*

## Some Questions You Might Ask

Is the soul solid, like iron?
Or is it tender and breakable, like
the wings of a moth in the beak of the owl?
Who has it, and who doesn't?
I keep looking around me.
The face of the moose is as sad
as the face of Jesus.
The swan opens her white wings slowly.
In the fall, the black bear carries leaves into the darkness.
One question leads to another.
Does it have a shape? Like an iceberg?
Like the eye of a hummingbird?
Does it have one lung, like the snake and the scallop?
Why should I have it, and not the anteater
who loves her children?
Why should I have it, and not the camel?
Come to think of it, what about the maple trees?
What about the blue iris?

What about all the little stones, sitting alone in the
   moonlight?
What about roses, and lemons, and their shining leaves?
What about the grass?

*Mary Oliver*

## Give Me a House

Give me a house, said Polly.
Give me land, said Hugh.
Give me the moon, said Sadie.
Give me the sun, said Sue.

Give me a horse, said Rollo.
Give me a hound, said Joe.
Give me fine linen, said Sarah.
Give me silk, said Flo.

Give me a mountain, said Kirsty.
Give me a valley, said Jim.
Give me a river, said Dodo.
Give me the sky, said Tim.

Give me the ocean, said Adam.
Give me a ship, said Hal.
Give me a kingdom, said Rory.
Give me a crown, said Sal.

Give me gold, said Peter.
Give me silver, said Paul.
Give me love, said Jenny,
Or nothing at all.

*Charles Causley*


# The Girl Who Made the Stars –
# a Bushman Story

The girl arose,
she put her hands into the wood ashes
and she said to them:
'Wood ashes
you must become the Milky Way
and lie along the sky
and go round with the stars
standing nicely round.'

And the girl threw the wood ashes up into the sky
and they became the Milky Way.

And the Milky Way gently glows
feeling that it is wood ashes

strewn along the sky
going round with the stars.

*Robert Hull*

# *Beginnings*

Perhaps all this

was shouted into being
by the sudden anger
of thunder

or sky
whet her fingers
in sprawled lakes
and sang the winds
across a flute

or the tree
of dark fell
and levered out
a root-face of white rock

or a frog
climbed to the top
of the pond of dark
and gulped out light

*Robert Hull*

# First Morning

I was there on that first morning of creation
when heaven and earth occupied one space
and no one had heard of the human race.

I was there on that first morning of creation
when a river rushed from the belly of an egg
and a mountain rose from a golden yolk.

I was there on the first morning of creation
when the waters parted like magic cloth
and the birds shook feathers at the first joke.

*John Agard*

# The Dawdling Dog
*from the West African Myth of Creation*

Said Chuku, Creator of the world
And everything in it,
My children will live forever
And thrive
But when they appear to die
They must lie on the ground
To be covered in ashes
And then they will revive.

Said Chuku to his new creation – Dog
Tell my children what to do
So that they will never die.
Go do as I bid.

But, dear child, the Dog dawdled
Dog dawdled
He did.

Said Chuku to his new creation – Sheep
Tell my children what to do
So that they will never die.
Go do as I ask.
But, quite frankly, Sheep wasn't up to the task
And, his thinking being rather woolly,
He said to the children of Chuku –
When you die, dig a hole
A hole for the dead.
And when the children asked why
Sheep said, It's good for the soul.

When Dog arrived late
And said to Chuku's children, No!
You must lay the dead on the ground
And cover them in ashes
And they will revive –
The children laughed and said,
Who are you trying to kid?
Sheep told us the truth.

And that is why
The children of Chuku
Grow old and die.
For Dog dawdled,
He dawdled
He did.

*Roger Stevens*

# Creation

God, smiling and chuckling
at His own designs.

Knee-deep in feathers and scales,
bits of beak and bone.

Elbows splattered with mud and sand,
clay and water, hair and fur.

Not so much the initial designs that impress,
original though they are.

It's what He did with the leftovers
that's real creative genius.

How else would you get an armadillo
or a duck-billed platypus?

*Paul Cookson*

# The Burning Bush

The bush blazed, brightly before Moses.
A voice came to him.
Take off your shoes said he.
Who are you? said Moses.
I am the God of this mountain said he.
Take off your shoes for this is Holy ground.
Moses came nearer no more.
He took off his shoes and knelt down before the bush.
The bush blazed like the white inside of the sun.
And yet Moses could see that the bush was unchanged.
Then God spoke one single word.
His name.
And power from God poured into Moses
As wine filling a cup.

*Deborah Blanchett, aged 8*

## *Some Other Ark*

Two by two
the animals everybody knows
          trotted, slithered,

hopped or were carried
          up Noah's gangplank.
But there was some other ark

          the unicorns chose:
an ill-pitched ark of bad gopher,
          an ark that leaked,

The man who sailed it couldn't
          smell or taste wind or rain
or see the Pole Star's crawl.

          He missed all olive leaves.
Drowned dragons, griffins, phoenixes
          and my precious unicorns.

                    *Fred Sedgwick*

## *Footprints in the Sand*

Footprints, footprints
Footprints in the sand
You and me Lord, on the beach
Walking hand in hand
Side by side you walk with me
Through this barren land
Footprints, footprints
Footprints in the sand

I look and see the footprints
Footprints in the sand
Two souls entwined together
God's walk along with man
Then I glance and see a sight
I don't quite understand
Just one set of footprints
Footprints in the sand

You said that you would be with me
I followed your command
But then you left me all alone
With pain that I could not withstand
The time I needed you the most
My Lord, I must demand
Why just one set of footprints
Footprints in the sand?

The Lord looked down and smiled
With gentle reprimand
*My son, this explanation*
*Everything is planned*
*I never left your side at all*
*And when you could not stand*
*That was when I carried you*
*Those footprints in the sand*

Footprints, footprints
Footprints in the sand
You and me Lord on the beach
Walking hand in hand
Often you would carry me
Through this barren land
Footprints, footprints
Footprints in the sand

*Paul Cookson*

# Who Is My Neighbour?

From Jerusalem to Jericho
the road was lonely, narrow, slow.

A man came walking down the track
as thieves crept up behind his back.

They knocked him down and beat his head
stripped him, robbed him, left for dead.

He lay there bleeding in the dirt
moaning, groaning, badly hurt.

The sun burned down, his throat ran dry
but then a priest came passing by.

'Water please,' cried out the man.
'Priest, help me any way you can.'

No help came, he was denied
the priest walked by on the other side.

A second priest ignored his plight
just walked away and out of sight.

As a Samaritan drew near
he shouted out in pain and fear,

'My wife and children will grieve for me
I am in the hands of my enemy.'

But with those hands his wounds were bathed
they raised him up and he was saved.

Carried as a donkey's load
to an inn along the road.

Washed and bandaged, laid to sleep
two silver coins left for his keep.

'Take care of him,' said his new friend,
'I'll pay whatever else you spend

And when he wakes let him know
I was his neighbour not his foe.'

*David Harmer*

## Jonah and the Whale

Well, to start with
It was dark
So dark
You couldn't see
Your hand in front of your face;
And huge
Huge as an acre of farmland.
How do I know?
Well, I paced it out
Length and breadth
That's how.
And if you was to shout
You'd hear your own voice resound,
Bouncing along the ridges of its stomach,
Like when you call out

Under a bridge
Or in an empty hall.
Hear anything?
No not much,
Only the normal
Kind of sounds
You'd expect to hear
Inside a whale's stomach;
The sea swishing far away,
Food gurgling, the wind
And suchlike sounds;
Then there was me screaming for help,
But who'd be likely to hear,
Us being miles from
Any shipping lines
And anyway
Supposing someone did hear,
Who'd think of looking inside a whale?
That's not the sort of thing
That people do.
Smell? I'll say there was a smell.
And cold. The wind blew in
Something terrible from the South
Each time he opened his mouth
Or took a swallow of some titbit.
The only way I found
To keep alive at all
Was to wrap my arms
Tight around myself
And race from wall to wall.

Damp? You can say that again;
When the ocean came sluicing in
I had to climb his ribs
To save myself from drowning.
Fibs? You think I'm telling you fibs,
I haven't told the half of it brother.
I'm only giving a modest account
Of what these two eyes have seen
And that's the truth on it.
Here, one thing I'll say
Before I'm done –
Catch me eating fish
From now on.

*Gareth Owen*

## The Call of St Francis

Come to me –
And bring me your truths.

Fish,
Swim to me;
Let your fins
Like softened seashells
Hear my call and bring
A lock of my hair,
Turned green by algae,

Sealed in your memory
Of plants and stones,
Forward to the sea of my making.

Bird,
Fly to me;
Let your wings
Feel my call and bring
The snap of your beak,
As sharp as the sound that you heard
When you broke into my world,
Forward to the tree of my making.

Animal,
Run to me.
Rabbit,
Let the spring uncoil and
Leap to me
With bent-back ears
Like ballerina's feet.

Snake,
Crawl to me
On your chess board stomach
And tell me the secrets of the ground.
Lion,
Run to me
With your mane of arrogance
And paws like clover leaves
And share your jungle with me.

Hear my call and bring to me
The space of your desert
Like the palm of my hand;
My sweat,
Your feverish heat.

Walk by my side
Or fly at my shoulder;
Swim at my feet
And give me your souls;
Make me whole with your stories of life
And make yourselves whole with mine.

*Leanora Dack, 13*

## Five Loaves and Two Fish

I had never been important,
never had the world turn and stare,
or ask 'Who's that over there?'
No, I was the quiet one in a crowd,
the small stone on a beach,
unsure, never proud,
but then I saw Jesus reach out
to me . . .
He asked 'Do you mind if I use it all?'
I watched the pieces of fish and bread
fall into baskets till they overflowed

and as I turned to go he said 'Thank you!
Everyone here has been fed.'
I went home, eager to tell friends the news . . .
What else do I have that Jesus might use?

*Mark Halliday*

## The Last Mountain

Once we mountains sported wings,
soared proud above the heavens,
frolicked among fleecy clouds
and slid up and down the rainbows
that groaned with our mighty weight.
Rushing wind was our element;
we played the music of the spheres.
The sky gifted us a giddy lightness
that stole the breath away.

But we took our freedom for granted
and jealous gods have clipped our wings.
Now distant thunder growls our grumbles
as my brothers and sisters tower in dreams
of how we once were monarchs of the air.
Yet I, the smallest of the mountains,
escaped the wrath of gods.
I hide in the frothing ocean and, sleepless,
I bide my time with folded wings.

The sea soil rumbles my secret songs
as I call to my family to take heart.
Their trust will strengthen me
and lift me up to strike a blow for our kind,
to fly up to the sun itself if need be,
to dance in our remembered freedom,
for faith, they say, moves mountains.

*Debjani Chatterjee*

## The Rainbow

'Make me a bow!'
said Indra
(God of Thunder, Lightning, Rain).
His carpenter raised his head.
'Make me a bow!'
Indra said –
the largest in the land
and my bow must be
the only one of its kind
in the whole Universe.

The carpenter hastened to obey
his mighty Master
and soon he made, of precious wood,
the largest bow that had ever been seen
in the whole Universe.

'Now paint my bow!'
said Indra
(God of Thunder, Lightning, Rain).
His artist – Visvakarma –
raised his head.
'Now paint my bow!'
Indra said –
In colours never known before
in the kingdom of the Gods.

So Visvakarma travelled down
from the Himalaya mountains in the north
to the deep green valleys of the south
to search for new colours
and when he found them
he began to paint the bow
in stripes.

For the first stripe he chose
Violet
the colour of the shimmery mist
at the top of the Himalaya mountains
at dawn.

The second stripe he painted
Indigo
the beautiful purpley-blue
that weavers coax out of the indigo plant
to dye their sun-bleached cloths.

For the third stripe he chose
Blue
the glistening blue
of the proud peacock's neck
as he dances in the rain.

The fourth stripe he painted
Green
the raw green of a young mango
before it turns ripe.

For the fifth he chose
Yellow
like the soft downy-fur
of a new-born lion cub.

The sixth stripe he painted
Orange
the colour of the dawn
like the stain of the mehndi plant
that decorates the hands and feet
of girls at festival time.

The seventh stripe was
Red
like the flaming ashoka flowers
in full bloom.

When Visvakarma had finished
he hung the bow out in the sky to dry

but the sun was too hot.
The bow began to bend and crack.
'God Indra!'
begged Visvakarma,
'It is too hot.
Let it rain a little, please.'

Indra looked at the bow of many colours
hanging in the sky
and he was pleased
so he –
'Let it rain a little.'

Visvakarma saw the colours
glowing through the rain
and he was happy.
'Do this every time you use your bow –
God Indra –
Hang it out when the sun is shining
through a little rain.
Then the wood will not crack
and the colours will remain fresh
forever.'

The God of Thunder, Lightning, Rain
took up his mighty bow
and smiled.
And since that day,
each time he uses
his bow of many colours,

he hangs it up in the sky
and children everywhere look up
and laugh
and shout –
'A Rainbow!'

*creation myth from India retold
by Beulah Candappa*

## Thirteen Things to Do with a Rainbow

Keep it for a skipping rope.
Throw it like a boomerang.
Put it on your head and wear it as a hair-band.
Climb to the top and slide down the other side.
Sew it into shirts and form Rainbow United Football Club.
Turn it upside down to make yourself a boat.
Pour each of its colours into seven biro-refills so you'll
    have a fresh pen for every day of the week.
Cut lengths of it to wrap up birthday presents for your
    favourite people.
Paint concrete, grey days and elephants with it.
Wear it as a scarf in winter.
Weave it into a strong rope to take on a dragon hunt.
Wind it round a disused lighthouse to make a helter
    skelter.
Don't let it out of your sight.

*David Horner*

## *How Fire Came to Earth*
### *Aboriginal legend*

In the Dream-Time, at the naming
Of the hills and trees and rivers,
Old Wakala sat in darkness,
Wished he had a fire to sit by,
Saw a blaze up in the heavens
Flashing brightly in the darkness
But the Karak-Karak snatched it,
Seven sisters, spirit-women,
Took it home and did not share it.
When the morning came the sisters
Fetched their bags to go out hunting.
Then Wakala called out to them,
'Come and eat your breakfast with me.
You and I will hunt together.'
After breakfast they went hunting
And Wakala watched the women,
Thinking he would steal their secret.
As they dug for roots and insects
With the pointed sticks they carried
Sparks went flying. Then Wakala
Knew the fire must be inside them.
After supper sly Wakala
Asked a question of the women.
'Sisters, which food is your favourite?'
'We eat most things,' said the sisters,
'Juicy termites are our favourite.

Only snakes are hateful to us.'
Then Wakala lay down, smiling.
Rising early, just as day broke,
He crept off and left them sleeping,
Looked for snakes and caught a bagful,
Found a termites' nest and quickly
Filled it with the writhing creatures.
Then he called the Karak-Karak –
'Come and see what I have found you!'
Seven sisters soon came running,
Saw the nest and tore it open!
Snakes leapt at them, hissing, squirming!
Terrified, the screaming women
Used their digging sticks as weapons,
Striking sparks upon the dry ground.
In an instant bold Wakala
Gathered up the glowing embers,
Ran away and left the sisters.
'Now the fire is mine!' he shouted,
Running, dancing like a madman.
All the snakes lay dead or dying
And the digging sticks were broken.
Then the wailing spirit-women
Felt the cold and could not bear it
So a wind came rushing, caught them
By the hair and whirled them upwards.
Seven shooting stars went flying
Up into eternal darkness.
Meanwhile, back on earth, Wakala
Made a fire and sat beside it.

Soon his neighbours came round begging
'Lend us fire to warm and cheer us.'
'Wah! Wah! Wah!' was all he answered,
'Go away! The fire is mine now.'
Then his neighbours turned against him,
Stoned Wakala, tried to kill him
But he picked up coals and flung them,
Setting clumps of dry grass blazing.
So the neighbours lit their torches,
Took them burning, flaming homeward.
'Wah! Wah! Wah!' complained Wakala,
Jumped into the fire to spite them.
Rising ghostly from the ashes
Came a crow with sooty feathers,
Cawing, calling in the daytime
'Wah! Wah! Wah!' While seven sisters
Shining brightly in the night-time
Tell the story over, over,
How fire came to earth in Dream-Time.

*Sue Cowling*

## Stars

Stars

are to reach for,
beautiful freckles of hope,
speckles on velvet,
to steer ships,
to comfort those trapped in the darkness of their making,
to lead the wayward when the compass falters,
to remind us that the day is almost breaking,
dawn is just out – taking time to warm the other side of
   the world.

Stars are for wishes.

Stars are
tiny lights of hope,
fireflies in the night,
golden specks to gaze at,
tin tacks on a dark cloth,
studs glittering,
sequins on a first party dress.

Stars are
our brightest and best,
shards of hope to keep us going,
marking the place,
marking the seasons,
giving us reasons

because somewhere out there

there are other star gazers
gazing back.

*Pie Corbett*

## Buddhist Prayer Flags and Wheels

Tiny coloured flags flutter
like rainbow leaves
muttering voiceless prayers –

Wheels spin and rattle,
battling with the wind,
sending out their messages of joy.

*Anon.*

## Thumbs Up

The emperor surveyed
The gladiators' fight –
When one was down
He gave a frown
And then displayed his might –

413

Thumbs up for life –
Thumbs down for death.

*Brian Duffy*


## Two Fingers

When the English
Captured French archers

They cut off their two bow fingers
So they could no longer shoot.

Then taunted their prisoners

Hooting,
Sneering and jeering,
Sticking two fingers
In a V
To remind them
Of what to their cost
They had lost.

Rude and crude –
The gesture still lasts,
Casting a handful of hate.

*Andrea Morgan*

# Chain-Song

If a jackal bothers you, show it a hyena,
If a hyena bothers you, show it a lion,
If a lion bothers you, show it an elephant,
If an elephant bothers you, show it a hunter,
If a hunter bothers you, show him a snake,
If a snake bothers you, show it a stick,
If a stick bothers you, show it a fire,
If a fire bothers you, show it a river,
If a river bothers you, show it the wind,
If the wind bothers you, show it God.

*Fulani*

# God in Everything

I am the wind which breathes upon the sea,
I am the wave of the ocean,
I am the murmur of the billows,
I am the ox of the seven combats,
I am the vulture upon the rocks,
I am a beam of the sun,
I am the fairest of plants,
I am a wild boar in valour,
I am a salmon in the water,
I am a lake in the plain,

I am a word of knowledge,
I am the God who creates in the head the fire.
Who is it that throws light into the meeting on the
　　mountain?
Who announces the ages of the moon?
Who teaches the place where couches the sun?

*Anon.*

## Where God Is Found

He is caught in anyone's fingers.
In Spring, he bursts out with the flowers.
At night he watches us all.
He is sensed in the scent of a flower.
He is heard in the rushing of the cool wind
and the running of clear water.
He is the touch of dawn
and the coming of daylight.
He is brighter than the sun rising.
He is seen in a brilliant flash of light.
He is grasped in the gleam of a dancer's hair.
In the Summer, his scent is of scarlet roses.
He is the taste of a chunk of chocolate.
He is heard in the swaying of apple trees in the wind
and in the crunch of a crisp apple.
He is seen in a mind.
He is held in the glint of a cat's eye.

In Autumn, he falls with the crinkly leaves
And sways in the sharp wind.
He sounds like church bells ringing all over town.
In Winter, he crunches like someone trudging in the snow.
He is the touch of a flower petal.
He is the sound of trumpets blowing in Heaven.
He is the rustle of reeds swaying in the wind.
He is in everyone and everything.

*Anna Budd, aged 8*

## To Find a Poem

To find a poem
listen to the wind
whispering words strange and rare
look under stones
there you might find a fossil
shape of an old poem.
They turn up anywhere
in the most unexpected places
look for words that are trapped
in the branches of trees
in the wings of birds
in rockpools by the sea.
And if you find one
handle it carefully
like an injured bird

417

for a poem can die
or slip through the fingers
like a live eel
and be lost in the stream.
Follow whatever footprints are there
even if no one else can see them
for clues to lost poems
are waiting to be found
round the next corner
or before you right now.
You may have just missed one
never mind
look again tomorrow
you may find your poem
or your poem
lost somewhere in the dark
may be waiting for you.

*Robert Fisher*


# Quiet

Be as still as you can
Feel the steady pulse of your heart
Like a bass guitar slowly thrumming
Drumming its beat.

Hear your blood

Pounding and pushing through your body
Gurgling rivers of red and blue
Giving you life.

Sense your breath
A rapidly shifting tide of air
Nose and mouth open
Lifting your lungs.

Clear your thoughts
As they rocket and race
Round the tunnels and tubes
Of your busy brain.

Be as still as you can
Hold this moment
Hold it once more, then rejoice
To know that today you're alive!

*David Harmer*

# Two Spanish Gypsy Lullabies

An angel of cinnamon
guards your cradle,
the head at the sun
the feet at the moon.

Under the laurels,
my daughter's cradle,
and when the moon rises
it calls her,
it calls her.

*Anon.*

# The Lord's Prayer

Our Father, which art in heaven,
Hallowed be thy name.
Thy kingdom come.
Thy will be done, in earth as it is in heaven.
Give us this day our daily bread.
And forgive us our trespasses
As we forgive them that trespass against us.
And lead us not into temptation
But deliver us from evil.
For Thine is the kingdom,
and the power, and the glory,
for ever and ever
Amen.

*Matthew 6:9–13*
*King James Bible*

# *Now may every living thing*

Now may every living thing, young or old, weak or strong, living near or far, known or unknown, living or departed or yet unborn, may every living thing be full of bliss.

*Buddha*

# Special Places

Lord make my heart a place where angels sing!

*John Keble*

## Reading in the Attic

At the top of the house
You can hear the feathered mutter
Of pigeons on the roof,
Or the gurgle of the gutter,
And the light shines yellow
Through the blinds like butter.

In this soft-sound space
In this gentle, golden air
I breathe the papery smell of books
And suddenly the 'where'
Of where I am dissolves
And I'm not here – I'm *there* . . .

Where time and space are folded
In the pages of a book,
And to travel anywhere or when
I only have to look,
Then be reeled in like a fish
On a shining story-hook.

*Jan Dean*

## *Playtent*

In my tent
The light is orange.
And I sit here
Still
As if I'm set in jelly.

It's magic here
In this golden space
Where a minute stretches on . . . and on . . . and on . . .

*Jan Dean*

## *Between My Two Worlds*

When I left London
I wrote of English summers
Of bluebells and blackbirds
And dreamt of the snow.

I came back to Scotland
And longed for the Monsoons
The flocks flying homewards
In the deep sunset glow.

My mother's concern, my father's care
My daughter's soft body that wasn't there;
So I switched my priorities and went back to stay
Carrying deep longings when I went away

To be enfolded in India
In its rich living spree
Yet turning to Britain
In my memory;

Till the unexpected happened
And my worlds switched again
To experience long daylight
And pine for the rain

Of a country burning
With the sun and my pain
Of living between two worlds
That I cannot maintain.

While my mother falters
And my father grows old
I hold *this* my country
As my daughter holds.

*Bashabi Fraser*

# The Bubble Between Two Buildings

Wet petals stick ragged pink splodges
on to the path
                        that twists and wriggles
under my feet like a long black snake.

The wind is warm, I can smell
blossom as it bends on its branches
watch it fly
                        in a shower of flowers
scattered into the rain spattering down.

I'm stuck in a bubble between two buildings
my arms full of registers, messages, parcels
all the classrooms
                        buzz like beehives full of bustle
children and grown-ups all painting and writing
talking and thinking, laughing and singing
chattering, shouting, counting and weighing.

Outside I can hear
the milk-float droning down our street
the other side of the fence
                        two dogs barking
and birds singing in the hedge by the path.

It's still and calm
breathing the blossom-heavy air
I lean into the warm, wet wind

                            wait for my feet
to lead me back to my busy classroom
down the shining tarmac painted with blossom.

*David Harmer*

## Riding the Chairlift

Stand still
Here on this high hill
And wait
While the man hooks and turns
The swinging chair.

Stand still
Until it creeps right up behind you
Then half-leap, half-hop
Hey-hup! Up!
Away into the air.

Below the earth shelves sharply
And suddenly we are sitting in the space of birdsong
Our shoes above the trees
Skimming above the sparrows.
Gliding to the quiet hum

Of wire and pulley. Slowly
Slowly now we come
Down over the wooded slopes
Where houses nestle in the trees
Like Lego bricks in broccoli.
The whole city is for dolls
And Matchbox toys.
There's no noise, no bustle
Only the great calm of the forest
And the strange creak of the chairlift
As we drift like slow snow
Down
Down
Down.

*Jan Dean*

## The View from my Window

Ali's built a den up in her attic,
Gary Farthing's got a gang hut in his father's shed,
Becky's built a bungalow in a nearby beech tree,
and Hassan has a hideaway where grown-ups dare not
    tread.

Inge's built an igloo out of used egg boxes,
Dougal's dug a dug-out beneath his parents' bed,
Tessa's made a tent out of blankets and a clothes-
    horse,
and Cecil has a cell in his cellar – so he's said.

Henry's headquarters are in his grandad's old wardrobe,
Jackie has a shack made from crates she's painted red,
Camara's made a lair in the cupboard under the stairs,
and me, I've a fully furnished universe . . .

here in my head . . .

instead.

*David Horner*

## Mr Khan's Shop

is dark and beautiful.
There are parathas,

garam masala,
nan breads full of fruit.

Shiny emerald chillies
lie like incendiary bombs.

There are bhindi in sacks,
aloo to eat with hot puris

and mango pickle. There's
rice, yoghurt,

cucumber and mint –
raitha to cool the tongue.

Sometimes you see
where the shop darkens

Mr Khan, his wife
and their children

round the table.
The smells have come alive.

He serves me
puppadums, smiles,

re-enters the dark.
Perhaps one day

he'll ask me to dine with them:
bhajees, samosas, pakoras,

coriander, dhall.
I'll give him this poem: *Sit down*

*young man*, he'll say
*and eat your words.*

Fred Sedgwick

## East Anglia

Wind whipping in from the sea.
Dunes. Grass so coarse it hurts. Larks
hammering tall spring air over crumbling coastlines.
    Views across fenland and heathland. A church like a
      liner

    where smiling angels hover.
Views across broadland in summer to barges
sewing sky/land seams. Clanking ferries, travellers' smiles.
    Towns smelling of malt and hop.

    Estuaries glinting like cheap jewellery.
No downs swinging deep into valleys and up to hilltops.
No steep paths dropping to tiny harbours. Men
    boasting fish just pulled from the Viking Sea.

*Fred Sedgwick*

## Riddles of the Seashore

Tossed into tangles by waves
it drizzles salt-sparkle on to sand.
       ?
Soft under seaweed the toe-nipper
waits for new armour.

?

Pentagram on the beach,
fish with a sky-name.

?

Not for collecting or poking,
leave this jellymould body for the tide.

?

In a bowl of barnacled rock a tiny sea
covers sea-flowers, shrimps and a crab.

?

Written in the sand, a seagull's poem
is rubbed out by waves.

?

As far as the eye can see, scallops
of white embroidery on grey-blue and blue-green.

?

Holding secret sea-songs and carried home,
it spills music into my ear.

?

*Catherine Benson*

## *Whitby Fragment*

The sea
swallows it all,
falls through itself
grinding stones to atoms:

moon caught in the foam
and thunder coming even
on a sunny day.

Meanings are worn down
constantly
under flat sunlight
glistening with salt,
years and pebbles
nothing but the same
mean nothing but the same –
beginnings and endings joined
in a twist of paper.

*Stephen Bowkett*

## Making the Countryside

Take a roll of green,
Spread it under a blue or blue-grey sky,
Hollow out a valley, mould hills.

Let a river run through the valley,
Let fish swim in it, let dippers
Slide along its surface.

Sprinkle cows in the water-meadows,
Cover steep banks with trees,
Let foxes sleep beneath and owls above.

Now, let the seasons turn,
Let everything follow its course.
Let it be.

*June Crebbin*


## Poem for Tamzin

Your neck of the woods was mine –
Where the whale-backed hills rolled green,
Where the busy spring buds burst,
Where May blossom speckled the hedgerows,
Where the hawk hung high,
Where the skylark dizzied itself in the blue spring air
And violets dotted downland paths.

Where the sun shimmered on tarmac,
Where the swallows dived in blue like tiny anchors,
Where clouds drifted by,
Where the trout flickered silver,
Where the dragonfly hovered,
Where the hedges smelled of thyme
And at night the moon hung like a bear's claw.

Where the winds shivered through the corn,
Where the leaves fell like a deck of cards,
Where chestnuts blossomed like tiny, green bombs,
Where apples blushed and raspberries fattened,
Where lightning crackled an electric vein,
Where lanterns lit in Hallowe'en windows
And pumpkins glowed like moons.

Where snow camouflaged the stone walls,
Where the sheep's wool froze on the barbed-wire fence,
Where puddles froze and the hills crouched,
Where the stars glittered and the fields turned to steel,
Where town lights strung out like a necklace,
Where the badger paused and caught my eye,
Where the winter sprung like a cold trap
And caught us in a cage of frost.

Yes, your neck of the woods was mine
When I was younger
And the world was so strong
That I could taste each day.

*Pie Corbett*

## Star Gazing

At midnight through my window
I spy with wondering eye
The far-off stars and planets
Sprinkled on the sky.

There the constant North Star
Hangs above our trees
And there the Plough and Sirius
And the distant Pleiades.

Star on star counting
Each one a raging sun
And the sky one endless suburb
With all her lights left on.

How strange it is that certain stars
Whose distant lights still glow
Vanished in that sea of space
Three million years ago.

And if I stare too long a time
The stars swim in my eyes
Drifting towards my bedroom
down the vast slope of the skies.

And, mesmerized, I wonder,
Will *our* Earth someday die?
Spreading her fabric and her dreams
In fragments on the sky.

And then my imagination
Sees in some distant dawn
A young girl staring skywards
On a planet still unborn.

And will she also wonder,
Was there ever life out there?
Before the whole thing vanished
Like a dream into the air.

*Gareth Owen*


## Heaven's Market

Sure, I dreamt of Heaven –
that market in the sky –
queues of smiling shoppers
all hoping they could buy

A brand new heart for grandad,
his old one can't keep time,
a zoo without the bars
where a cage would be a crime.

Some sharp eyes for my auntie,
her old ones both wore thin,
new shoes that never tire
and some races you can win.

Fresh Ethiopian rain,
a dad for Cushla too,
books that read themselves
and a sky that's always blue.

A stranger's smile that means it,
a pet that cannot die,
balloons that never burst
bright words that never lie.

*Pie Corbett*

## Puja in Brixton

The hall echoes –

the pine floor shines.

Incense drifts
and candles flicker.

Sitting cross-legged,
my knees ache.

We meditate
watching our thoughts float by
like clouds
easing through the mind's sky.

Together we chant –
our hundred voices
becoming one.

Touching my brow
on the floor,
placing my heart
above my mind.

Prasad –
we sip sweet tea
and chew chocolate biscuits.

*Ali Baker*

Puja is another word for worship

## Here's the Church

Here is the church,
Here is the steeple,
Open the doors,
And here are the people.
Here's the parson going upstairs,
And here he is saying his prayers.

*Anon.*

## Cathedral

Come into this quiet place where
Angels carved in stone look down on
Tombs of noble lords and ladies.
Here are stained-glass windows to delight the
Eye and tell us tales of long ago – here the Great West
Door and there an eagle spreads its wings. Here are
Rows and rows of seats and high above each aisle
Arches soar. Come into this quiet place.
Listen to its peace.

*June Crebbin*

## Liverpool Cathedral

It's like standing in God's waiting room
Gazing up at an indoors sky
At the shadows high above
Hoping to glimpse a soul
My thoughts
Adrift in that universe
Of smooth brown Woolton sandstone

I feel like a fish
Trying to grab a strand
Of weed
That's floating on the sea's surface
With hands I do not possess

*Roger Stevens*

## Early Morning, Bradford

Frost glitters
on grey pavements.

The red-bricked terrace
hunches the hill-side.

A wintry wind
grips the streets,

slips down backyards

till shy sunlight
slyly catches the mosque

and its golden dome
gleams!

Joy sparks
amongst cold grey –
welcoming the day.

*Pie Corbett*


## Prayer

The place is full of worshippers.
You can tell by the sandals
piled outside, the owners' prints
worn into leather, rubber, plastic,
a picture clearer than their faces
put together, with some originality,
brows and eyes, the slant
of cheek to chin.

What prayer are they whispering?
Each one has left a mark,
the perfect pattern of a need,
sole and heel and toe
in dark curved patches,
heels worn down,
thongs ragged, mended many times.
So many shuffling hopes,
pounded into print,
as clear as the pages of holy books,
illuminated with the glint
of gold around the lettering.

What are they whispering?
Outside, in the sun,
such a quiet crowd
of shoes, thrown together
like a thousand prayers
washing against the walls of God.

*Imtiaz Dharker, Pakistan*

## The Summer-House

My summer-house
Is white with lime,
And roses climb
About the door,

And columbines
And gentle lady-flowers,
And fuchsias
And the carmine fairy-cap.
And rose-mallow
And red crow-toes,
And the fringed jessamine.
All day long
On the thorn before the door
The mellow blackbird pipes;
And thither echoes come
Of the long low wash of the sea,
And of the shy call
Of the hill-plover on the hill,
And of the plaintful song
Of the turf-cutters in the bog.

Oh, my house
Is a house of happiness,
My house
Is a house of love.

*Joseph Campbell*

## Secret Country
*(from* The Pied Piper*)*

There is no money
So there's no crime
There are no watches
Cos there's no time
It's a good country
It's a secret country
And it's your country and mine

If something's needed
You make it there
And we have plenty
For we all share
It's a kind country
It's a secret country
And it's your country and mine

There are no cages
There is no zoo
But the free creatures
Come and walk with you
It's a strange country
It's a secret country
And it's your country and mine

There are no prisons
There are no poor
There are no weapons
There is no war
It's a safe country
It's a secret country
And it's your country and mine

And in that country
Grows a great tree
And it's called Freedom
And its fruit is free
In that blue country
In that warm country
In that loving country
In that wild country
In that secret country
Which is your country and mine

*Adrian Mitchell*


# Cardboard Box

I've got this box
and it's all mine
I pop in there
from time to time

It's like a camp
or hideaway
a secret place
that's out the way

It's where I go
to be alone
it's safe in there
a tiny home

My cardboard box
I love it lots

*James Carter*


## School Creed

This is our school.
Let peace dwell here,
Let the rooms be full of contentment,
Let love abide here,
Love of one another,
Love of mankind,
Love of life itself,
And love of God.
Let us remember
That, as many hands build a house,
So many hearts make a school.

*Anon.*

# from *How Should I Praise Thee, Lord!*

Whether I flie with angels, fall with dust,
Thy hands made both, and I am there:
Thy power and love, my love and trust
Make one place ev'rywhere.

*George Herbert*

# Festival Dates of Different Faiths

| | Christian | Jewish | Hindu | Sikh | Buddhist |
|---|---|---|---|---|---|
| **Month** | | | | | |
| **January** | New Year (1 Jan) Epiphany (6 Jan) | | | | |
| **February** | Lent (Feb–April) Shrove Tuesday St Valentine's (14 Feb) | | | | |
| **March** | St David's (1 March) St Patrick's (17 March) | Passover (Mar–April) | Holi (Feb–Mar) | | Purim (Feb–Mar) |
| **April** | All Fools' Day (1 April) Easter: Palm Sunday Maundy Thursday Good Friday (Mar–April) St George's (23 April) | | | Baisakhi | New Year |
| **May** | May Day Ascension | | | | Buddha's enlightenment Wesak (May–June) |

## Festival Dates of Different Faiths

| | Christian | Jewish | Hindu | Sikh | Buddhist |
|---|---|---|---|---|---|
| **Month** | | | | | |
| **June** | Pentecost | | | | Buddha's Cremation |
| **July** | | | | | |
| **August** | | | | | |
| **September** | | Rosh Hashana | | | |
| **October** | | | Divali (Oct–Nov) | | |
| **November** | | | | Guru Nanak's birthday | Kathina Ceremony Festival of lights |
| **December** | Advent (Nov–Dec) Christmas (25 Dec) Boxing Day (26 Dec) | Hanukkah | | | All Saints' Day |

The Muslim festivals, including Ramadan and Eid, follow a lunar calendar and so fall on dates that vary from year to year.

# Index of First Lines

453

# Index of Poets

# Index of Poets

465

# Acknowledgements

The compiler and publisher would like to thank the following for permission to use copyright material:

**Catherine Benson**, 'The Chinese Dragon' from *Poems about Festivals*, ed. A.F. Peters, Hodder Wayland (2000), 'Easter Monday' from *Frogs in Clogs*, ed. Gaby Morgan, Macmillan (2005), 'Fostered' from *I Love My Mum*, ed. Gaby Morgan, Macmillan (2006), 'Walking Home with My Foster Father' from *Reflecting Families*, ed. J. Chernaik, BBC Education (1995), and 'Riddles of the Seashore' from *The Universal Vacuum Cleaner*, ed. John Foster, OUP (2005), all by permission of the author; **Gerard Benson**, 'Spring Assembly' and 'A Small Star' from *To Catch An Elephant*, poems by Gerard Benson, Smith/Doorstop (2002), and 'Winter, Goodbye' first published in *Mice on Ice*, ed. Gaby Morgan, Macmillan (2004), all by permission of the author; **James Berry**, 'Benediction', 'One', 'A Nest Full of Stars' and 'Childhood Tracks' all by permission of the author; **Clare Bevan**, 'Last Day' and 'First Day' first published in *The School Year*, ed. Brian Moses, Macmillan (2001), 'Rainbow Rice' first published in *The Poetry Store*, ed. Paul Cookson, Hodder (2005), 'Listen' first published in *Christmas Poems*, ed. Gaby Morgan, Macmillan (2003), and 'The Bully', 'What Will You Do?', 'Boscastle, 2004', 'Touching the Cat', 'The Pebble' and 'Magic Wand' all by permission of the author; **Stephen Bowkett**, 'Menagerie', 'How to Explore the Universe', 'I Am the Wizard!' and 'Whitby Fragment' all by permission of the author; **Liz Brownlee**, 'April 1st' by permission of the author; **Dave Calder**, 'Dragon' and 'Summer Afternoon' both by permission of the author; **James Carter**, 'First Day' and 'Cardboard Box' first published in *Hey Little Bug!*, Hands Up Books (2006), 'The Dark', 'Sulky in St Ives' and 'A Map of Me' from *Cars Stars Electric Guitars* by James Carter, Walker Books Ltd (2002), 'Happy Poem', 'Write Your Name', 'Love You More', 'Amazing Inventions', 'Big Mother', 'The Big Things' and 'Road' first published in *Time-Travelling Underpants*, Macmillan (2007), and 'Let It Go' by permission of the author; **Debjani Chatterjee**, 'Mela Menagerie' and 'Diwali' from *Animal Antics* by Debjani Chatterjee, Pennine Pens (2000), 'An "Indian Summer"' from *Daughters of a Riverine Land*, Sahitya Press (2003), 'Mehndi Time' from *Masala: Poems from India, Bangladesh, Pakistan and Sri Lanka*, Macmillan (2005), 'If' first appeared on www.bbc.co.uk/jam (2006), 'The Last Mountain' from *Namaskar: New and Selected Poems* by Debjani Chatterjee, Redbeck Press (2004), and 'Eid Mubarak!' by permission of the author; **Mandy Coe**, 'Sensing Mother' from *Sensational!*, ed. Roger McGough, Macmillan (2004), and 'Assembled' by permission of the author; **John Coldwell**, 'Bully', 'Agreement', 'Best Friends (Not)' and 'Setting Off' all by permission of the author; **Paul Cookson**, 'I

# Acknowledgements

Think I'm the Only One', 'The Longest Day of the Year', 'Prayer for the First Day of the School Holidays', 'A Christmas Meditation (Prayer)', 'These Are the Hands', 'Actions Speak', 'May You Always', 'Let No One Steal Your Dreams', 'You Never Say Sorry First', 'Full of Surprises', 'Just Mum and Me', 'Father's Hands', 'Together', 'Mum and Dad Are Mum and Dad', 'Brother's Best at Sandcastles', 'Fishing with Uncle John', 'With You, Without You', 'Never', 'Bullies and Their Messengers', 'Invisible Magicians', 'First and Lasting Impressions', 'Losing at Home', 'Chantha', 'Mwajuma Wants to Return Home', 'Three-Minute Silence, Three Minute Poem', 'Creation', 'Footprints in the Sand' all by permission of the author; **Sue Cowling**, 'Ass', 'Christening Gift', 'What to Do When Angry', 'Our Sounds', 'Marjorie', 'You Find Out Who Your Friends Are', 'For Now', 'What I Like About Ice', 'Looking Forward' and 'How Fire Came to Earth' all by permission of the author; **Brian D'Arcy**, 'Hold Fast' by permission of the author; **Jan Dean**, 'Easter' from *The Poetry Store*, ed. Paul Cookson, Hodder (2005), 'It's Not What I'm Used To', 'Reading in the Attic', 'Playtent' and 'Riding the Chairlift' from *Wallpapering the Cat*, Macmillan (2003), 'Nothing That Lives Is Ever Lost' from *Trick or Treat*, ed. Paul Cookson, Macmillan (2005), 'Temptation' from *A Mean Fish Smile*, Cowling, Dean and Stevens, Macmillan (2000), 'Dedicating a Baby' from *The Works 2*, ed. Brian Moses and Pie Corbett, Macmillan (2002) and 'Be Tall, Thomas' all by permission of the author; **Penny Dolan**, 'Half-Term' by permission of the author; **Gina Douthwaite**, 'Mad March Sun' by permission of the author; **Eric Finney**, 'First Star' and 'The View from Space' from *Space Poems*, ed. Gaby Morgan, Macmillan (2006), and 'Finding Magic' from *The Works 2*, ed. Brian Moses and Pie Corbett, Macmillan (2002), all by permission of the author; **John Foster**, 'Recipe for a Summer Holiday' from *Four O'Clock Friday* by John Foster, OUP (1991), 'On New Year's Eve' and 'In My Dream' from *Climb Aboard the Poetry Plane*, OUP (2000), 'It Hurts', 'Pride Comes Before a Fall' and 'The Shell' from *Making Waves* by John Foster, OUP (1997), and 'Not the Answer', 'Sarah, My Sister, Has Asthma', 'Where Is the Forest?', 'I Dream of a Time' and 'Christmas 1992' from *Standing on the Sidelines* by John Foster, OUP (1995), all included by permission of the author; **David Harmer**, 'A Prayer for Lent', 'One Moment in Summer', 'All of Us Knocking on the Stable Door', 'Hopes', 'Dobbo's First Swimming Lesson', 'Mister Moore', 'Our Tree', 'Catching October Leaves', 'Floodwaters', 'The News', 'The Prime Minister Is Ten Today', 'Who Is My Neighbour?', 'Quiet' and 'The Bubble Between Two Buildings' all by permission of the author; **David Horner**, 'A Pupil's Prayer' and 'Thirteen Things to do with a Rainbow' from *Mmmmmm*, Apple Pie Publications, and 'The View from My Window' from *So There!*, Apple Pie Publications, all by permission of the author; **Jenny Joseph**, 'Great sun' from *All the Things I See*, Macmillan (2000), and 'There Are Too Many . . .' and 'The Magic of the Brain' from *Extreme of Things*, Bloodaxe Books (2006), all by permission of the author; **Jackie Kay**, 'Word of a

# Acknowledgements

Lie' and 'The Want-Want Twins' from *The Frog Who Dreamt She Was an Opera Singer*, Bloomsbury, both by permission of the author; **Jean Kenward**, 'Mela' and 'Stepmother' both by permission of the author; **John Kitching**, 'No More' by permission of the author; **Rupert M. Loydell**, 'No One Made Mash Like My Grandad!' and 'Full' both by permission of the author; **Kevin McCann**, 'Questions' by permission of the author; **Ian McMillan**, 'The Music I Like' and 'New Day' from *The Invisible Villain*, Macmillan (2002), both by permission of the author; **Lindsay MacRae**, 'The Funeral' by permission of the author; **Tony Mitton**, 'Hunting the Leaven' by permission of the author; **John Mole**, 'Remembrance Day Remembered' from *The Wonder Dish* by John Mole, OUP (2002); **Brian Moses**, 'Distributing the Harvest' and 'Names' from *Knock Down Ginger and other poems*, CUP (1994), and 'The Lost Angels' from *Don't Look at Me in that Tone of Voice*, Macmillan (1998), all by permission of the author; **Chris Ogden**, 'The Minister of Awe and Wonder' by permission of the author; **Gareth Owen**, 'Wedding Day', 'Jonah and the Whale' and 'Star Gazing' all by permission of the author; **Brian Patten**, 'Remembering Snow' and 'Small Wonders' from *Thawing Frozen Frogs*, Puffin (1992), both by permission of the author, c/o Rogers, Coleridge and White; **Gervase Phinn**, 'A Parent's Prayer' and 'Lizzie's Road' both by permission of the author; **Joan Poulson**, 'Wilderness' by permission of the author; **Janis Priestley**, 'Just One Wish (feeling full of joy)' by permission of the author; **John Rice**, 'Seaside Song' from *Zoomballoomballistic*, Aten Press (1982) and 'Big Fears' from *Rockets and Quasars*, Aten Press (1984), both by permission of the author; **Coral Rumble**, 'Sorry' from *Poems About Me*, ed. Brian Moses, Wayland (1998), 'A Visit to Casualty' from *Breaking the Rules* by Coral Rumble, Lion (2004), and 'The First Bit' from *The Rhyme Riot*, ed. Gaby Morgan, Macmillan (2002), all by permission of the author; **Vernon Scannell**, 'Contradictions of Love', 'The Power of Love' and 'Getting There' all by permission of the author; **Fred Sedgwick**, 'Loving Gertie Best' from *Jenny Kissed Me*, ed. Fred Sedgwick, Questions (2000), 'Lord of All Gardens' from *Will there Really Be a Morning?*, ed. Fred Sedgwick, David Fulton (2002), 'When I Was Angry', 'First Thing Today' and 'Mr Khan's Shop' from *Blind Date* by Fred Sedgwick, Tricky Sam (1991), 'Kelly Jane Dancing' from *Pizza Curry Fish and Chips*, Longman (1994), and 'Cinquain Prayer, February Night', 'Teacher's Prayer, September', 'Elegy for Bonfire Night', 'Song for a Birthday', 'East Anglia' and 'Some Other Ark', all by permission of the author; **Ian Souter**, 'My Dad Is Amazing!' by permission of the author; **Roger Stevens**, 'Mother's Day Prayer' and 'The Estuary Field Trip' from *A Mean Fish Smile*, Macmillan (2000), 'End of Term' from *On My Way to School I Saw A Dinosaur*, Hands Up Books (2005), 'Christmas Morning' from *The Big Book of Christmas*, ed. Gaby Morgan, Macmillan (2005), 'Night Puzzle', 'What's My Name?', 'The You Can Be ABC' and 'Shelley' from *Never Trust a Lemon*, Rabbit Press, 'The Most Important Rap' from *Performance Poems*,

# Acknowledgements

Southgate, 'Prayer', 'Silent Song', 'Stone' and 'A Time to Be Silent' from *I Did Not Eat the Goldfish*, Macmillan, and 'The Dawdling Dog' and 'Liverpool Cathedral' all by permission of the author; **Nick Toczek**, 'The Dragon Who Ate Our School' from *Dragons*, Macmillan (2005), and 'Rowdy Kids' both by permission of the author; **John Whitworth**, 'The Cheer-up Song' by permission of the author; **Kit Wright**, 'Mercy' and 'Grandad' both by permission of the author.

Every effort has been made to trace the copyright holders, but if any have been inadvertently overlooked then the publishers will be pleased to make the necessary arrangement at the first opportunity.